LEVEL 2 Supplemental

ULTIMATE MUSIC THEORY

By Glory St. Germain ARCT RMT MYCC UMTC &
Shelagh McKibbon-U'Ren RMT UMTC

The LEVEL 2 Supplemental Workbook is designed to be completed with the Prep 2 Rudiments Workbook.

GSG MUSIC

Enriching Lives Through Music Education

ISBN: 978-1-927641-43-9

 # The Ultimate Music Theory™ Program

The Ultimate Music Theory™ Program lays the foundation of music theory education.

The focus of the Ultimate Music Theory Program is to simplify complex concepts and show the relativity of these concepts with practical application. This program is designed to help teachers and students discover the excitement and benefits of a sound music theory education.

The Ultimate Music Theory Program is based on a proven approach to the study of music theory that follows the *"must have"* Learning Principles to develop effective learning for all learning styles.

The Ultimate Music Theory™ Program and Supplemental Workbooks help students prepare for nationally recognized theory examinations including the Royal Conservatory of Music.

Respect Copyright - Copyright 2017 Gloryland Publishing
All rights reserved. No part of this publication may be reproduced or transmitted in any form or by any means, electronic or mechanical, including photocopying, recording, or any information storage and retrieval system, without permission in writing from the author/publisher.

* Resources - An annotated list is available at UltimateMusicTheory.com under Free Resources.

GSG MUSIC

Library and Archives Canada Cataloguing in Publication
UMT Supplemental Series / Glory St. Germain and Shelagh McKibbon-U'Ren

Gloryland Publishing - UMT Supplemental Series:

GP-SPL	ISBN: 978-1-927641-41-5	UMT Supplemental Prep Level
GP-SL1	ISBN: 978-1-927641-42-2	UMT Supplemental Level 1
GP-SL2	ISBN: 978-1-927641-43-9	UMT Supplemental Level 2
GP-SL3	ISBN: 978-1-927641-44-6	UMT Supplemental Level 3
GP-SL4	ISBN: 978-1-927641-45-3	UMT Supplemental Level 4
GP-SL5	ISBN: 978-1-927641-46-0	UMT Supplemental Level 5
GP-SL6	ISBN: 978-1-927641-47-7	UMT Supplemental Level 6
GP-SL7	ISBN: 978-1-927641-48-4	UMT Supplemental Level 7
GP-SL8	ISBN: 978-1-927641-49-1	UMT Supplemental Level 8
GP-SCL	ISBN: 978-1-927641-50-7	UMT Supplemental Complete Level

Ultimate Music Theory
LEVEL 2 Supplemental

Table of Contents

Ultimate Music Theory	The Story of UMT… Meet So-La & Ti-Do	4
Comparison Chart	Level 2	6
Three Ledger Lines	Treble Staff and Bass Staff	8
Grand Staff	Same Pitch, Different Staff	10
Scale Degrees	Tonic, Subdominant, Dominant and Leading Tone	11
Scale Degrees	Leading Tone or Subtonic	12
Roman Numerals	Functional Chord Symbols	13
Tonic Major Triad	Functional Chord Symbols - Major key	14
Tonic Minor Triad	Functional Chord Symbols - minor key	16
Triad Quality	Major and minor, Root/Quality Chord Symbols	18
Chord Symbols	Root/Quality Chord Symbols - Major & minor scales	20
Major or Minor	Functional Chord & Root/Quality Chord Symbols	22
Music Theory Game	Climb Tonic Mountain (Root/Quality Chord Symbols)	23
Musical Terms & Signs	Repeat Signs, Prefix Terms, Pedals	24
Melody Writing	Ending on Stable Scale Degrees ($\hat{1}$ or $\hat{3}$)	26
Melody Phrase Ending	Unstable or Stable Scale Degrees	28
ICE & Analysis	Imagine, Compose, Explore - Baby Butterfly	30
Music History	Wolfgang Amadeus Mozart - Symphony and Opera	32
Listening Activity	Twelve Variations (K 265) Twinkle, Twinkle, Little Star	34
Concerto and Rondo	Movements and Form	36
Listening Activity	Horn Concerto No. 4 in E flat Major (K 495) Third Movement	38
Rhythm Review	Tap with Ti-Do	39
Theory Exam	Level 2	42
Certificate	Completion of Level 2	48

Score: **60 - 69** Pass; **70 - 79** Honors; **80 - 89** First Class Honors; **90 - 100** First Class Honors with Distinction

Ultimate Music Theory: *The Way to Score Success!*

Workbooks, Exams, Answers, Online Courses, App & More!

A Proven Step-by-Step System to Learn Theory Faster - from Beginner to Advanced.

Innovative techniques designed to develop a complete understanding of music theory, to enhance sight reading, ear training, creativity, composition and musical expression.

All UMT Series have matching Answer Books!

The UMT Rudiments Series - Beginner A, Beginner B, Beginner C, Prep 1, Prep 2, Basic, Intermediate, Advanced & Complete (All-In-One)

♪ 12 Lessons, Review Tests, and a Final Exam to develop confidence
♪ Music Theory Guide & Chart for fast and easy reference of theory concepts
♪ 80 Flashcards for fun drills to dramatically increase retention & comprehension

Rudiments Exam Series - Preparatory, Basic, Intermediate & Advanced

♪ 8 Exams plus UMT Tips on How to Score 100% on Theory Exams

Each Rudiments Workbook correlates to a Supplemental Workbook.

The UMT Supplemental Series - Prep Level, Level 1, Level 2, Level 3, Level 4, Level 5, Level 6, Level 7, Level 8 & Complete (All-In-One) Level

♪ Form & Analysis and Music History - Composers, Eras & Musical Styles
♪ Melody Writing using ICE - Imagine, Compose & Explore
♪ 12 Lessons, Review Tests, Final Exam and 80 Flashcards for quick study

Supplemental Exam Series - Level 5, Level 6, Level 7 & Level 8

♪ 8 Exams to successfully prepare for nationally recognized Theory Exams

UMT Online Courses, Music Theory App & More

♪ UMT Certification Course, Teachers Membership & Elite Educator Program
♪ Ultimate Music Theory App correlates to the Rudiments Workbooks
♪ Free Resources - Teachers Guide, Music Theory Blogs, videos & downloads

Go To: UltimateMusicTheory.com

Ultimate Music Theory

At Ultimate Music Theory we are passionate about helping teachers and students experience the joy of teaching and learning music by creating the most effective music theory materials on the planet!

Introducing the Ultimate Music Theory Family!

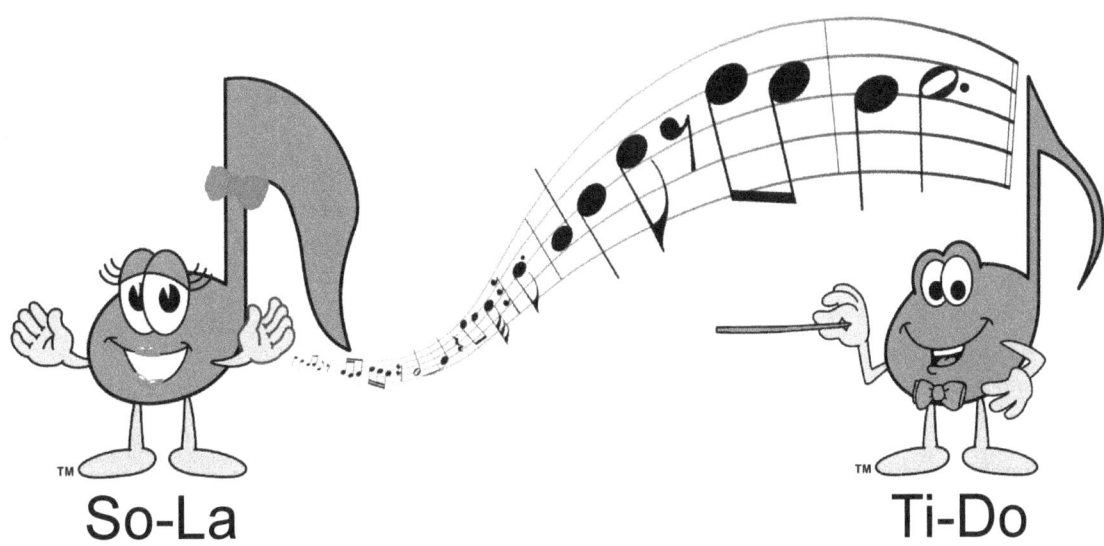

So-La

Meet So-La! So-La loves to sing and dance.

She is expressive, creative and loves to tell stories through music!

So-La feels music in her heart. She loves to teach, compose and perform.

Ti-Do

Meet Ti-Do! Ti-Do loves to count and march.

He is rhythmic, consistent and loves the rules of music theory!

Ti-Do feels music in his hands and feet. He loves to analyze, share tips and conduct.

So-La & Ti-Do will guide you through Mastering Music Theory!

Enriching Lives Through Music Education

The Ultimate Music Theory™ Comparison Chart to the 2016 Royal Conservatory of Music Theory Syllabus.
Level 2

The Ultimate Music Theory™ Rudiments Workbooks, Supplemental Workbooks and Exams prepare students for successful completion of the Royal Conservatory of Music Theory Levels.

UMT Prep 2 Rudiments Workbook plus the LEVEL 2 Supplemental = RCM Level 2.
♪ Note: Additional completion of the LEVEL 3 Supplemental Workbook = RCM Theory Level 3.

RCM Level 2 Theory Concept | Ultimate Music Theory Prep 2 Workbook

Required Keys:
- C, G, F Major; a, e, d minor

Keys Covered:
- C, G, D, F, B-flat Major; a, e, b, d, g minor

Pitch and Notation:
- Notes up to and including three ledger lines above and below the Treble & Bass Staff
- Stems and beams

Pitch and Notation Covered:
- Notes up to and including two ledger lines
- Stems, beams, flags and dots
*Workbook Pages - Three Ledger Lines (Treble, Bass and Grand)

Rhythm and Meter
- Notes: dotted quarter notes
- Time Signatures: 2/4, 3/4 and 4/4
   - bar lines, notes and rests

Rhythm and Meter Covered
- Notes: dotted quarter notes and eighth notes (single/beamed)
- Time Signatures: 2/4, 3/4 and 4/4 bar lines, notes, pulses & rests
*Workbook Pages - Rhythm Review - Tap with Ti-Do

Intervals
- Half Steps - using same or different letter names
- Whole Steps
- Melodic and Harmonic intervals up to and including an octave (numerical size only)

Intervals Covered
- Half Steps/Semitones - using same or different letter names
- Whole Steps/Whole Tones
- Melodic and Harmonic intervals up to and including an octave (numerical size only)

Scales and Scale Degree Names
- Scales using Key Signatures and/or Accidentals:
  - C Major, G Major and F Major
  - natural form: a minor, e minor, d minor
  - harmonic form: a minor, e minor, d minor
- Relative Major/minor Key Relationships
- Scale degree numbers ($\hat{1} - \hat{8}$)
- Tonic, Subdominant, Dominant and Leading Note

Scales and Scale Degree Names Covered
- Scales using Key Signatures and/or Accidentals:
  - C Major, G Major, D Major, F Major and B-flat Major
  - natural form: a minor, e minor, b minor, d minor and g minor
  - harmonic form: a minor, e minor, b minor, d minor and g minor
- Relative Major/minor Key Relationships and Circle of Fifths
- Scale degree numbers ($\hat{1} - \hat{8}$)
- Tonic, Supertonic, Mediant, Subdominant and Dominant
* Workbook Pages - Leading Tone and Subtonic

Chords
- Tonic Triads of required keys in Root Position (solid/blocked or broken form)
- Functional Chord Symbols (I, i)
- Root/Quality Chord Symbols (ex. C, Am)

Chords Covered
- Tonic Triads of required keys in Root Position (solid/blocked or broken form) *Game - Climb Tonic Mountain
*Workbook Pages - Functional Chord Symbols
*Workbook Pages - Root/Quality Chord Symbols

* Supplemental Workbook Pages - New concepts introduced in the 2016 RCM Syllabus.

UltimateMusicTheory.com © Copyright 2017 Gloryland Publishing. All Rights Reserved.

RCM Level 2 Theory Concept (Continued)

Melody and Composition

- Composition of a short melody in a Major Key with a given rhythm.
  - Use steps and skips.
  - End on scale degree $\hat{1}$ or $\hat{3}$.

Analysis

- Identification of concepts from this level and the previous levels within short music examples.
- Identification of melodic phrases.

Musical Terms and Signs

- Tempo, Dynamics and Articulation

Music History/Appreciation

- An Introduction to Mozart

- Twelve Variations on "Ah vous dirai-je, Maman" ("Twinkle, Twinkle, Little Star") K 265 by Mozart
  - Listening focus - changes to the theme (example: melody, rhythm, accompaniment)

- Horn Concerto No. 4 in E flat Major, K 495, Third Movement: Rondo by Mozart
  - Listening focus - overall shape and design (return of opening theme)

Examination
(No Level 2 Theory Exam)

Ultimate Music Theory Prep 2 Workbook (Continued)

Melody and Composition Covered

*Workbook Pages - Motive - Rhythmic Pattern and Melodic Pattern, Recurring Motive, Melody Writing - Ending on Stable Scale Degrees ($\hat{1}$ or $\hat{3}$), using steps and skips
*Workbook Pages - Phrase Ending - Unstable ($\hat{2}$ or $\hat{7}$) or Stable ($\hat{1}$ or $\hat{3}$) Scale Degrees

Analysis Covered

*Workbook Pages -- Identification of concepts from this level and the previous level within short music examples
* Workbook Page - Analysis, Terms and Sight Reading

Musical Terms and Signs Covered

*Workbook Pages - Musical Terms and Signs

Music History/Appreciation Covered

*Workbook Pages - Life and Music of Wolfgang Amadeus Mozart

*Workbook Pages - Mozart, Symphony and Opera
*Workbook Pages - Listening focus to the Twelve Variations on "Ah vous dirai-je, Maman" ("Twinkle, Twinkle, Little Star") K 265 (melody, rhythm, accompaniment)

*Workbook Pages - Concerto and Rondo Form
*Workbook Pages - Listening focus to the Horn Concerto No. 4 in E flat Major, K 495, Third Movement: Rondo by Mozart (overall shape and design, including return of opening theme)

Review Tests & Final Exam

- 12 Accumulative Review Tests (1 with each of the 12 Lessons)
*UMT LEVEL 2 THEORY EXAM

UltimateMusicTheoryApp.com - Over 7000 Flashcards including audio! 6 Subjects: Beginner - Prep, Basic, Intermediate, Advanced, Ear Training & Music Trivia (including History).

Beginner Music Theory App Subject - Use with the Prep 1 and Prep 2 Workbooks

12 Decks - 1,325 Cards - See, hear and identify notes on the staff, scales, triads and musical terms. Learn notation including note and rest values, Key Signatures, 4/4 Simple Time & more!

1 - Notation, Landmarks and Ledger Lines	2 - Note & Rest Values and Intervals
3 - Simple Time Signatures	4 - Semitones, Whole tones & Accidentals
5 - Major scales - 2 sharps & 2 flats	6 - Natural minor scales - 2 sharps & 2 flats
7 - Key Signatures - 2 sharps & 2 flats	8 - Key Signatures on the Grand Staff
9 - Major Triads - solid and broken	10 - Harmonic minor scales
11 - Melodic minor scales	12 - Analysis and Musical Terms

THREE LEDGER LINES - TREBLE STAFF (Use after Prep 2 Rudiments Page 13)

Ledger lines are short lines used to extend the staff as needed for notes written above or below the Treble Clef. Ledger lines must be equal distance from the staff.

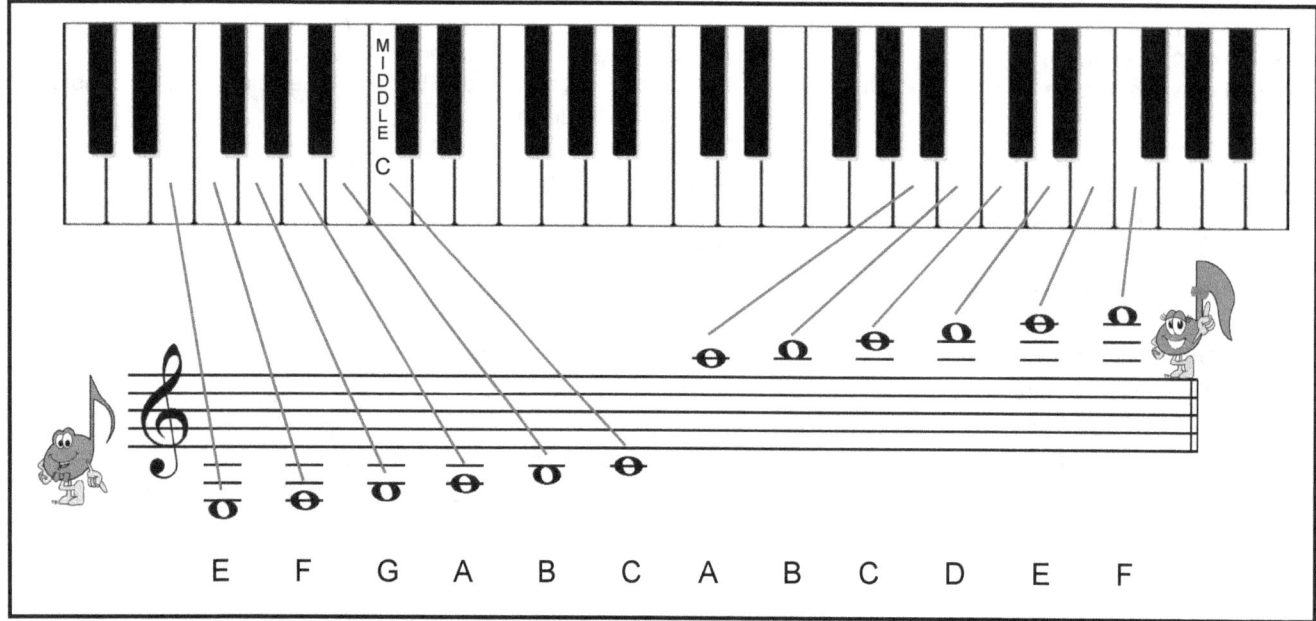

1. Write the following notes. Use ledger lines. Use whole notes.

   a) ABOVE the Treble Clef. b) BELOW the Treble Clef.

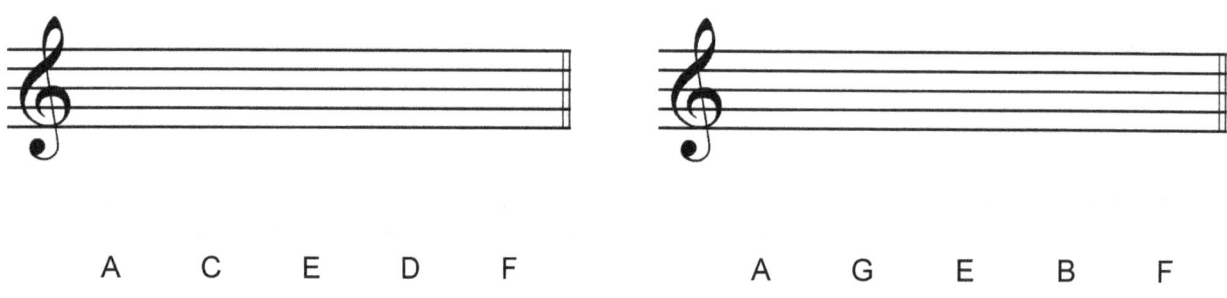

2. Name the following notes in the Treble Clef.

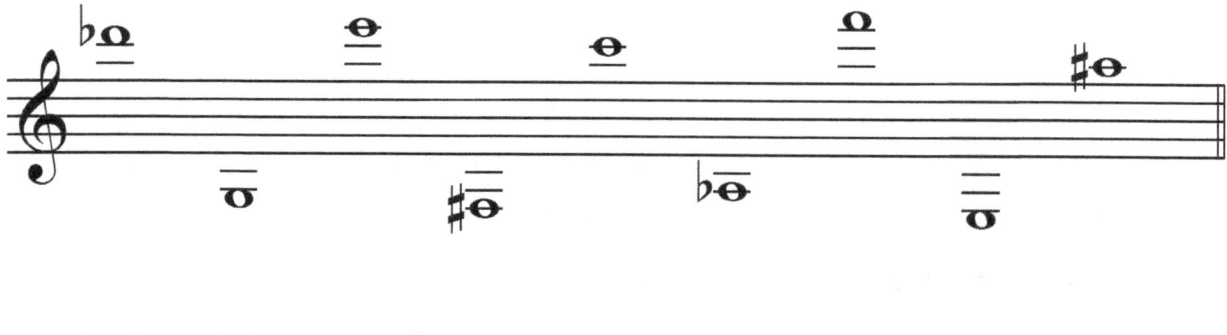

THREE LEDGER LINES - BASS STAFF (Use after Prep 2 Rudiments Page 13)

Ledger lines are short lines used to extend the staff as needed for notes written above or below the Bass Clef. Always use your UMT Ruler to draw straight ledger lines.

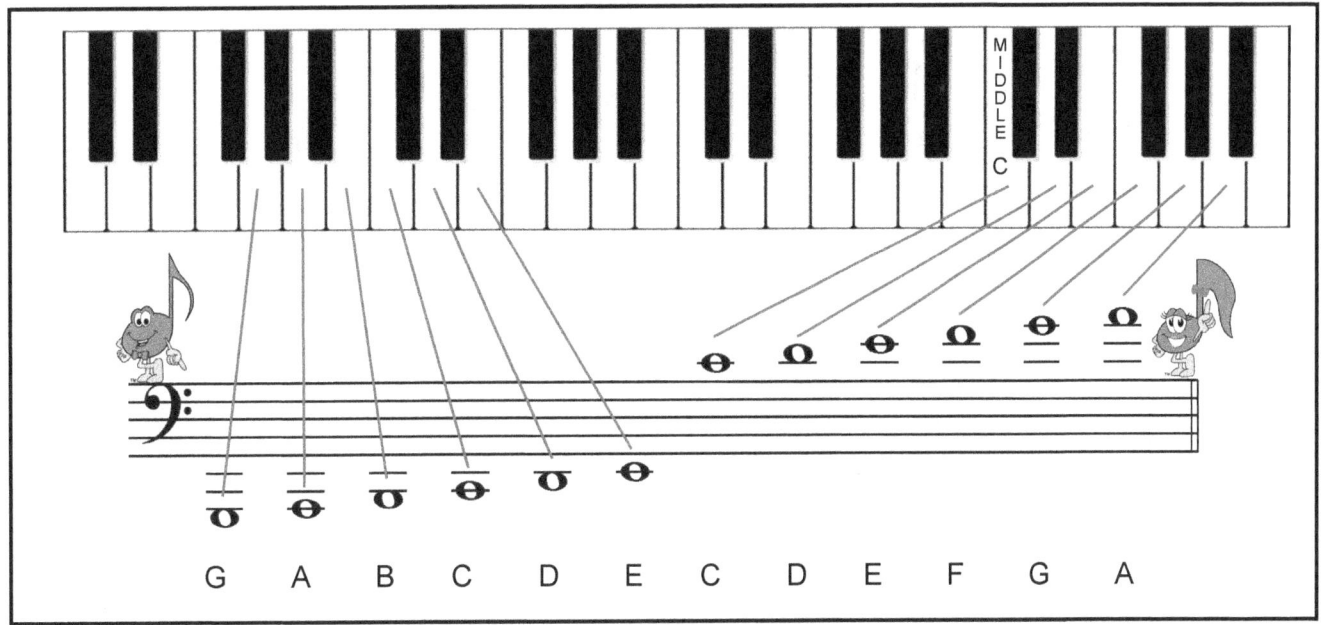

1. Write the following notes. Use ledger lines. Use whole notes.

   a) ABOVE the Bass Clef.   b) BELOW the Bass Clef.

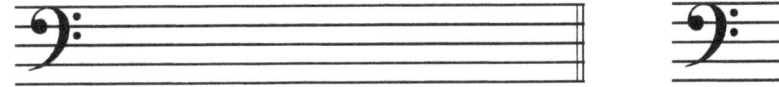

A F D G E   A C E G B

2. Name the following notes in the Bass Clef.

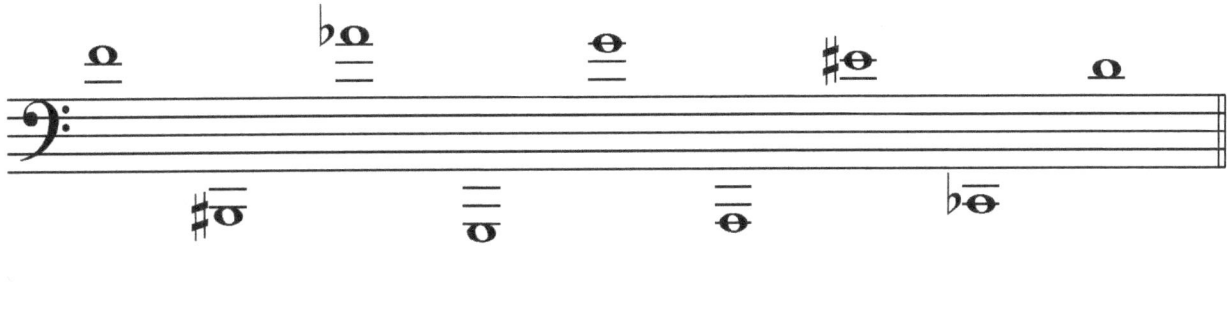

GRAND STAFF - SAME PITCH, DIFFERENT STAFF (Use after Prep 2 Rudiments Page 13)

Using ledger lines, notes can be written at the **SAME PITCH** in the Treble Staff and in the Bass Staff. Always use your UMT Ruler to draw straight ledger lines.

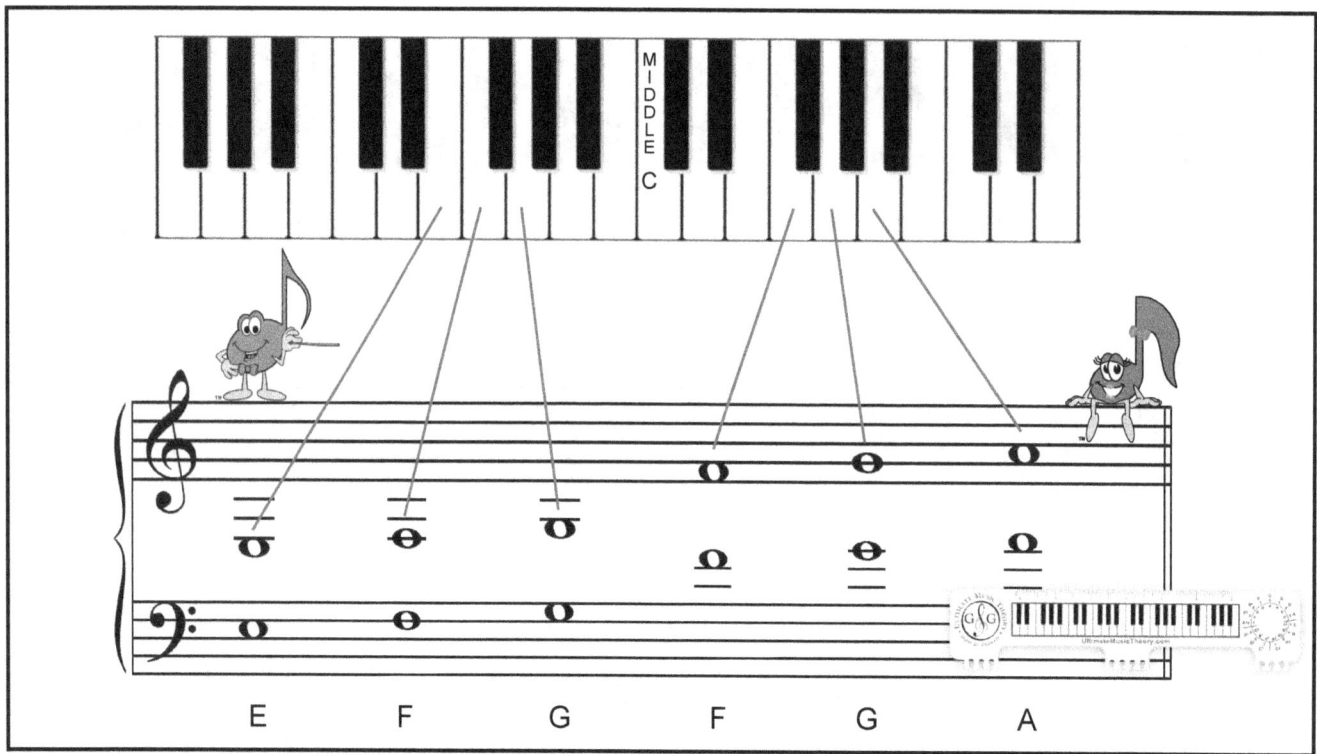

1. a) Name the following notes.
   b) Draw a line from each note to the corresponding key on the keyboard (at the correct pitch).

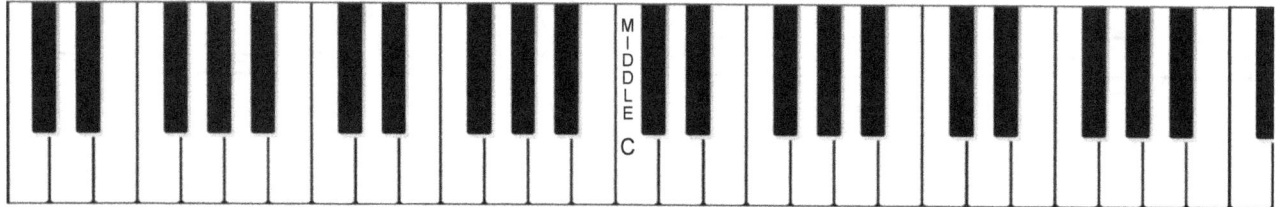

SCALE DEGREE NAMES - TONIC, SUBDOMINANT, DOMINANT and LEADING TONE
(Use after Prep 2 Rudiments Page 73)

Scale Degree Names begin with the starting note ($\hat{1}$, or first note) of the Scale called the **Tonic**. The ending note or last note $\hat{8}$ ($\hat{1}$) of the Scale is also called the Tonic as it uses the same letter name.

The fourth note ($\hat{4}$) of the Scale is called the **Subdominant**.

The fifth note ($\hat{5}$) of the Scale is called the **Dominant**.

The seventh note ($\hat{7}$) of the Major Scale and the Harmonic Minor Scale is called the **Leading Tone**. The Leading Tone (or Leading Note) is always a half step (semitone) below the Upper Tonic ($\hat{8}$).

So-La Says:

The Subdominant $\hat{4}$ is a fifth below the Upper Tonic.

The Dominant $\hat{5}$ is a fifth above the Lower Tonic.

The Leading Tone $\hat{7}$ is a half step (semitone) below the Upper Tonic.

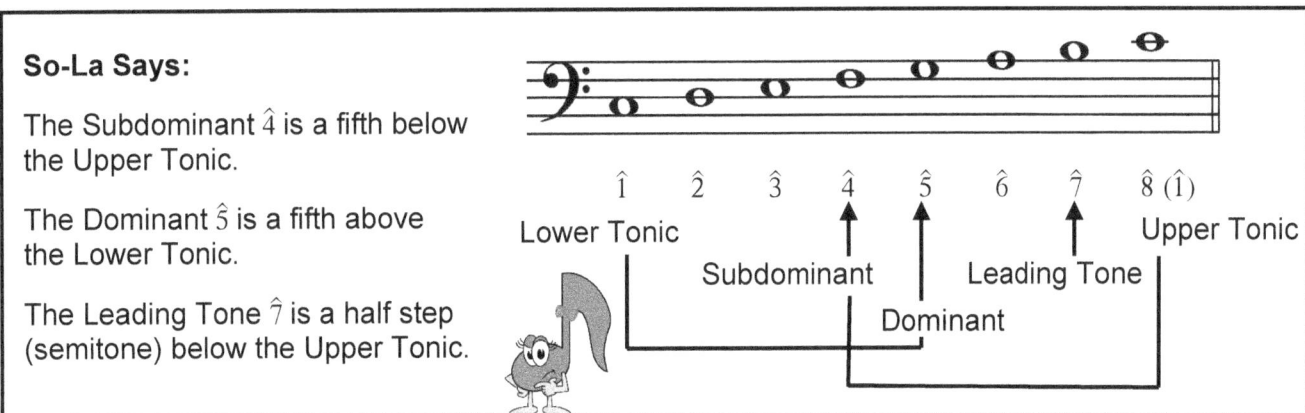

1. Below each scale, label each Tonic (T), Subdominant (SD), Dominant (D) and Leading Tone (LT).

   a) G Major scale

   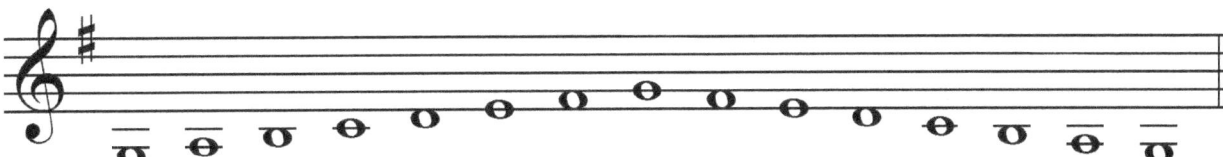

   b) d minor harmonic scale

   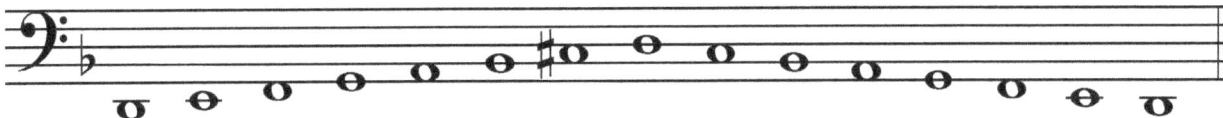

♪ **Ti-Do Time:** LISTEN as your Teacher plays the scales in Exercise 1.

Identify if the scale played is the G Major scale or the d minor harmonic scale.

SCALE DEGREES - LEADING TONE or SUBTONIC (Use after Prep 2 Rudiments Page 104)

The seventh note ($\hat{7}$) of the Major Scale and the Harmonic Minor Scale is called the **Leading Tone**.
The Leading Tone (LT) is always a half step (semitone) below the Upper Tonic ($\hat{8}$).

The seventh note ($\hat{7}$) of the Natural Minor Scale is called the **Subtonic**.
The Subtonic (SBT) is always a whole step (whole tone) below the Upper Tonic ($\hat{8}$).

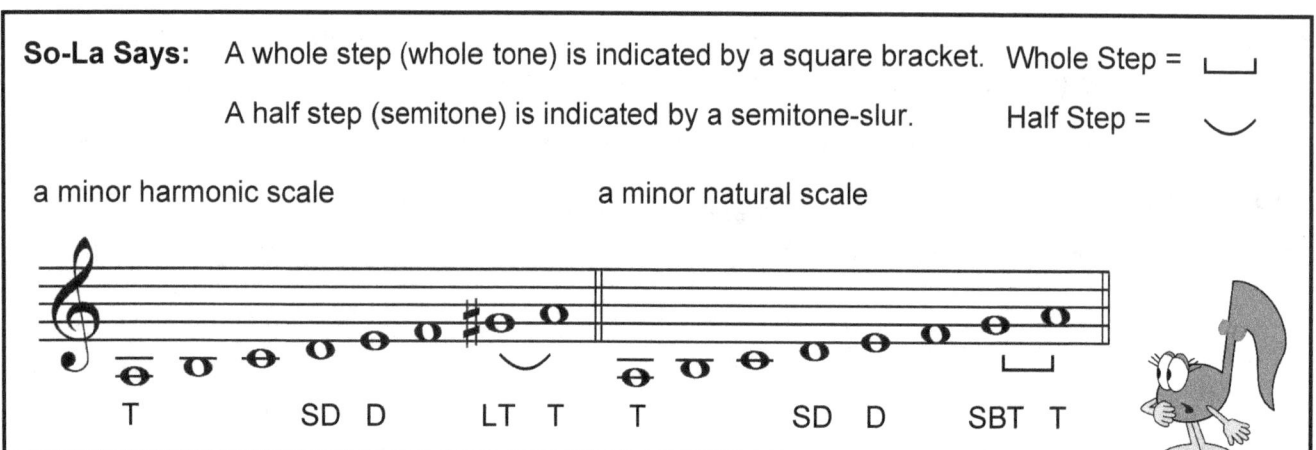

♫ **Ti-Do Tip:** A scale written with a center bar line will repeat accidentals in the descending scale.

A scale written without a center bar line will only use accidentals in the ascending scale.

1. a) The e minor harmonic scale below is written using a center bar line. Label each Tonic (T), Subdominant (SD), Dominant (D) and Leading Tone (LT).
   b) Indicate the distance between the Leading Tone and the Upper Tonic with a semitone-slur.

2. a) The e minor natural scale below is written without a center bar line. Label each Tonic (T), Subdominant (SD), Dominant (D) and Subtonic (SBT).
   b) Indicate the distance between the Subtonic and the Upper Tonic with a square bracket.

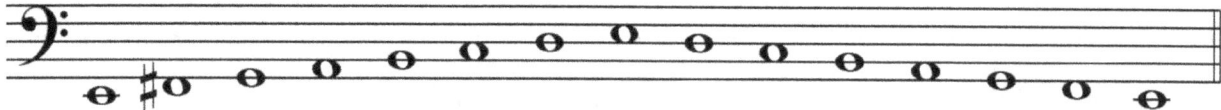

FUNCTIONAL CHORD SYMBOLS (Use after Prep 2 Rudiments Page 104)

Functional Chord Symbols are **Roman Numerals** (I, i, II, ii, III, iii, IV, iv, V, v, etc.) that indicate the scale degree number of the note and the quality (Major or minor sound) of the triad built on that note.

Functional Chord Symbols (Roman Numerals) are always written below the triad and below the staff.

So-La Says:	Functional Chord Symbols		
The **Functional Chord Symbol** Chart shows how to write the Major or minor Roman Numeral for each triad quality. **Major Triad** = Uppercase Roman Numeral **Minor Triad** = Lowercase Roman Numeral	Scale Degree Number	Uppercase (Major) Roman Numeral	Lowercase (minor) Roman Numeral
	8 (1̂)	VIII (I)	viii (i)
	7̂	VII	vii
	6̂	VI	vi
	5̂	V	v
	4̂	IV	iv
	3̂	III	iii
	2̂	II	ii
	1̂	I	i

♪ **Ti-Do Tip:** A triad built on the Tonic (1̂) of the Major scale is a Major triad. It has a happy sound.

A triad built on the Tonic (1̂) of the minor scale is a minor triad. It has a sad sound.

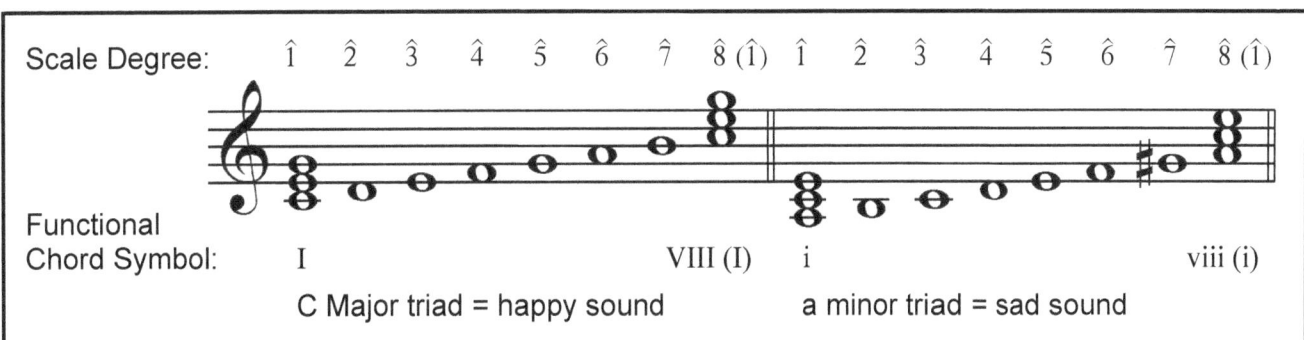

C Major triad = happy sound   a minor triad = sad sound

1. Circle the correct Functional Chord Symbol for each of the following triads.

   a) The C Major triad built on Scale Degree 1̂ uses the Roman Numeral: I   or   i

   b) The a minor triad built on Scale Degree 1̂ uses the Roman Numeral: I   or   i

♪ **Ti-Do Time:**   LISTEN as your Teacher plays the solid triads in the second Example box.

Identify if the triad played is the C Major triad or the a minor triad.

UltimateMusicTheory.com © Copyright 2017 Gloryland Publishing. All Rights Reserved. 13

FUNCTIONAL CHORD SYMBOL - MAJOR TRIAD (Use after Prep 2 Rudiments Page 104)

The **Functional Chord Symbol** (Roman Numeral) of the triad built on the Tonic of the Major scale is I.

The Triad built on the Tonic (1̂) of the Major scale is always a **Major triad**, I (a happy sound).

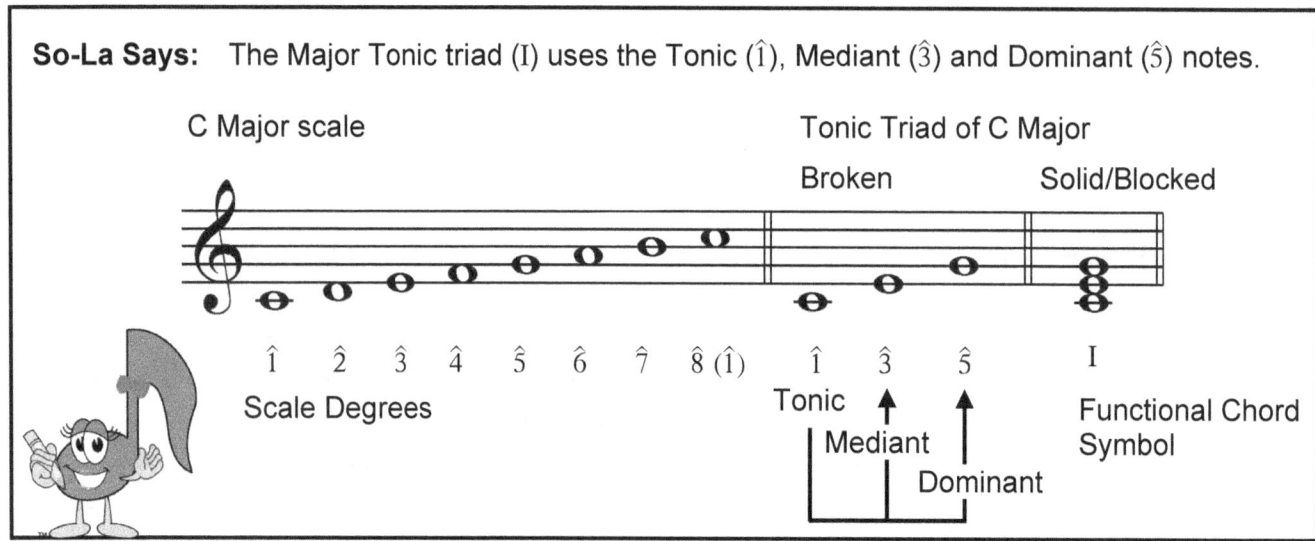

♫ **Ti-Do Tip:** The Functional Chord Symbol (I) is written below the Staff.

1. For each of the following Major scales:
   a) In Measure 1, write the scale, ascending, one octave. Use a Key Signature. Use whole notes.
   b) In Measure 2, write the notes of the Tonic triad, broken ascending. Use whole notes.
   c) In Measure 3, write the notes of the Tonic triad, solid/blocked. Use whole notes.

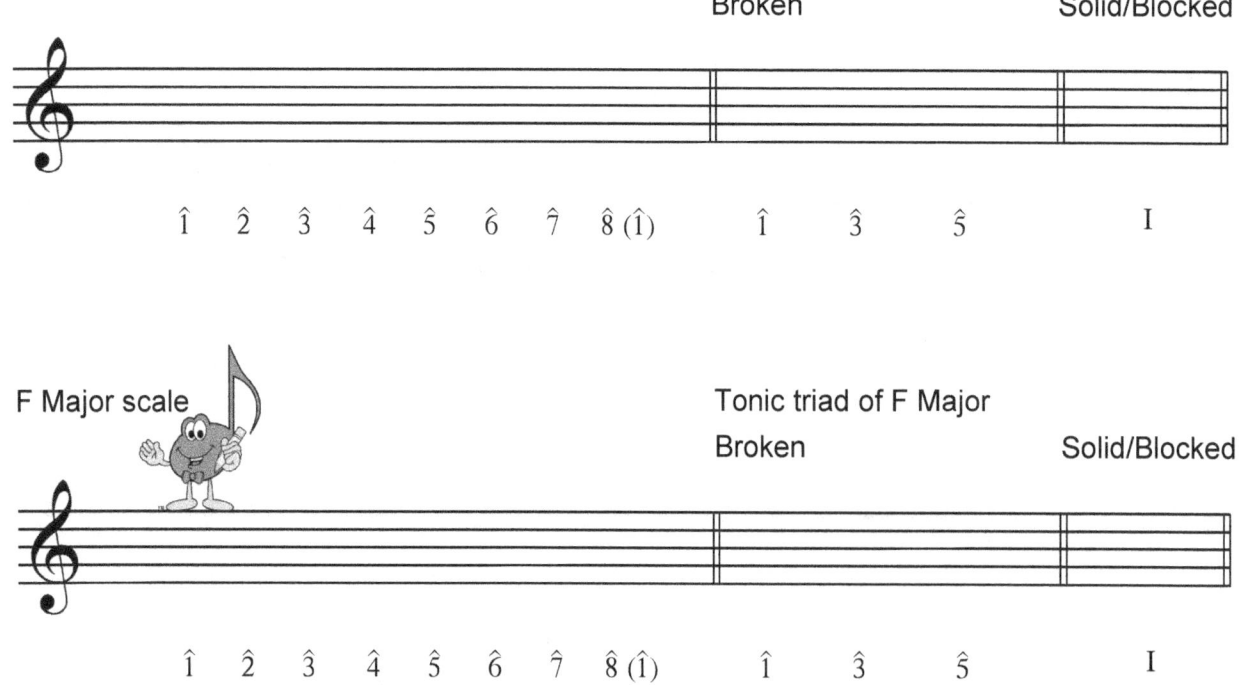

FUNCTIONAL CHORD SYMBOL - TONIC TRIAD - MAJOR KEY (Use after Prep 2 Page 104)

The **Functional Chord Symbol** for the **Tonic triad** of a **Major key** is I.

The Functional Chord Symbol, Roman Numeral I, is written below the first note of the triad.

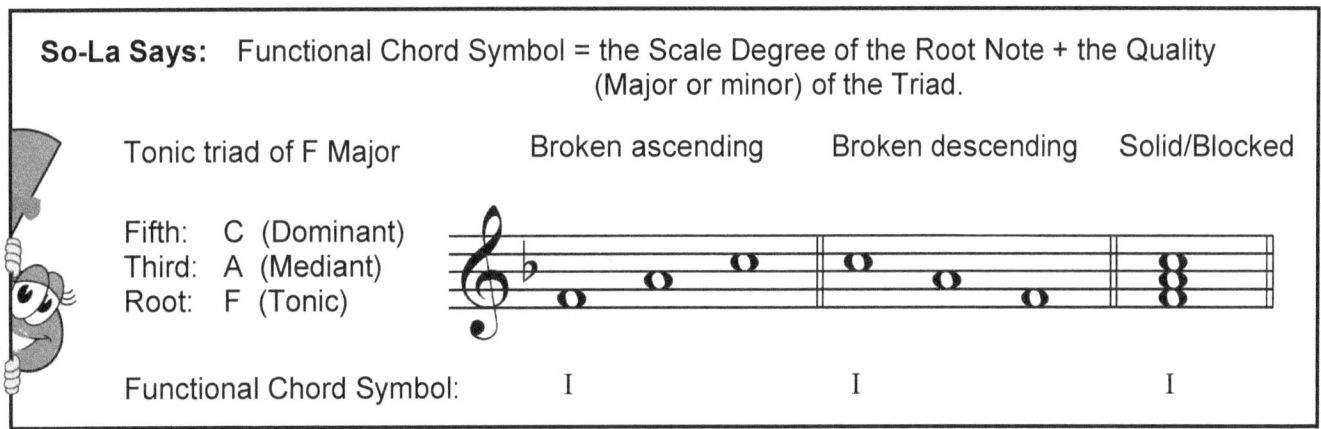

So-La Says: Functional Chord Symbol = the Scale Degree of the Root Note + the Quality (Major or minor) of the Triad.

Tonic triad of F Major — Broken ascending — Broken descending — Solid/Blocked

Fifth: C (Dominant)
Third: A (Mediant)
Root: F (Tonic)

Functional Chord Symbol: I   I   I

1. For each of the following Major key Tonic triads:
   a) Name the Third (Mediant) and the Fifth (Dominant) above the Root (Tonic).
   b) In Measure 1, write the notes of the broken ascending Tonic triad. Use whole notes.
   c) In Measure 2, write the notes of the broken descending Tonic triad. Use whole notes.
   d) In Measure 3, write the notes of the solid/blocked Tonic triad. Use whole notes.

Tonic triad of G Major   Broken ascending   Broken descending   Solid/Blocked

Fifth: _____

Third: _____

Root: __G__

Functional Chord Symbol: I   I   I

Tonic triad of C Major   Broken ascending   Broken descending   Solid/Blocked

Fifth: _____

Third: _____

Root: __C__

Functional Chord Symbol: I   I   I

♫ **Ti-Do Time:** LISTEN as your Teacher plays the Major Tonic triads in Exercise 1. Identify the triad as broken ascending, broken descending or solid.

FUNCTIONAL CHORD SYMBOL - MINOR TRIAD (Use after Prep 2 Rudiments Page 104)

The **Functional Chord Symbol** (Roman Numeral) of the triad built on the Tonic of the minor scale is i.

The Triad built on the Tonic ($\hat{1}$) of the minor scale is always a **minor triad**, i (a sad sound).

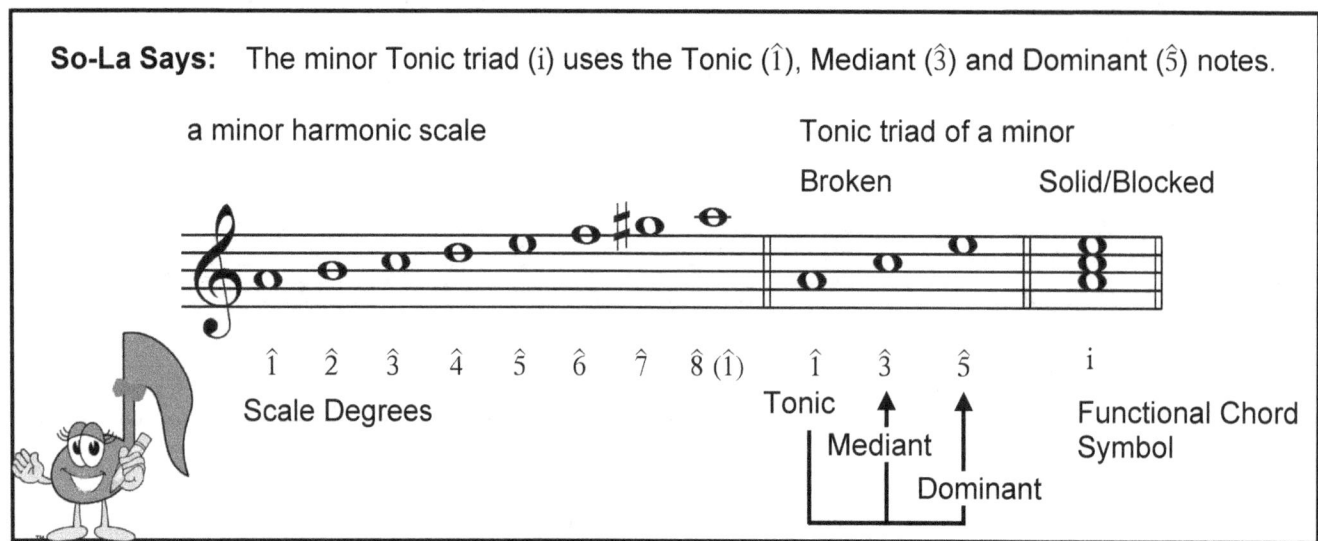

♪ **Ti-Do Tip:** The Functional Chord Symbol (i) is written below the Staff.

1. For each of the following minor harmonic scales:
    a) In Measure 1, write the scale, ascending, one octave. Use a Key Signature. Use whole notes.
    b) In Measure 2, write the notes of the Tonic triad, broken ascending. Use whole notes.
    c) In Measure 3, write the notes of the Tonic triad, solid. Use whole notes.

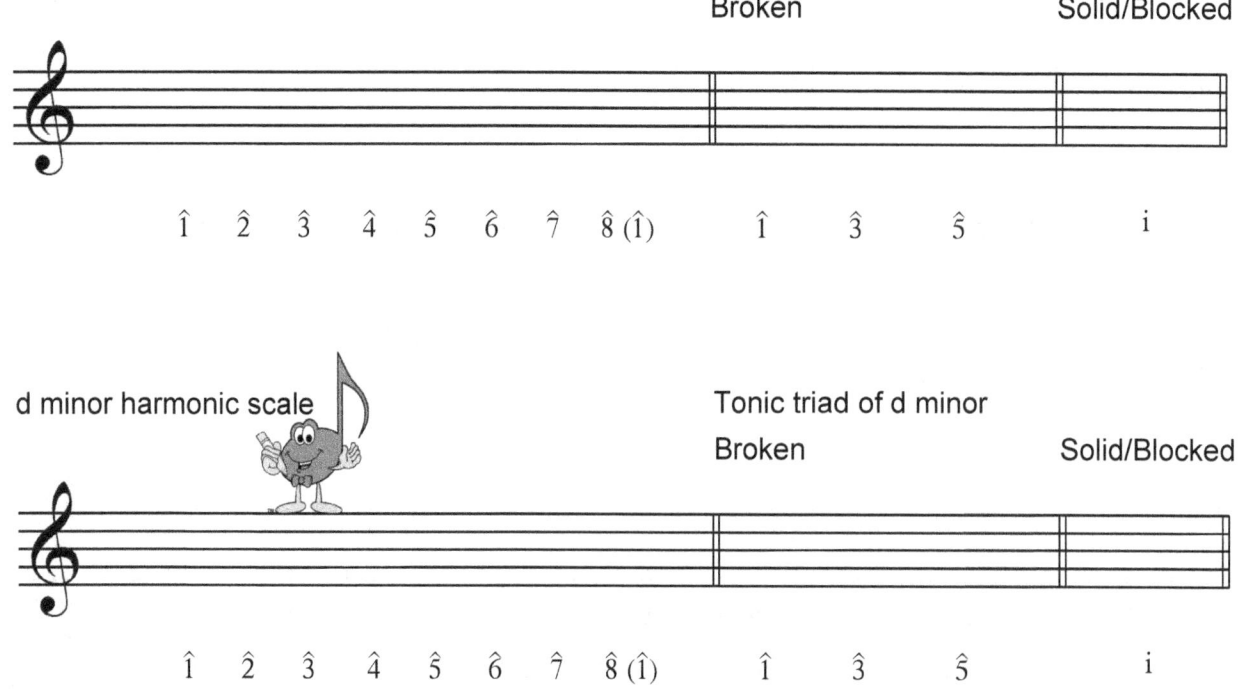

FUNCTIONAL CHORD SYMBOL - TONIC TRIAD - MINOR KEY (Use after Prep 2 Page 104)

The **Functional Chord Symbol** for the **Tonic triad** of a **minor key** is i.

The Functional Chord Symbol, Roman Numeral i, is written below the first note of the triad.

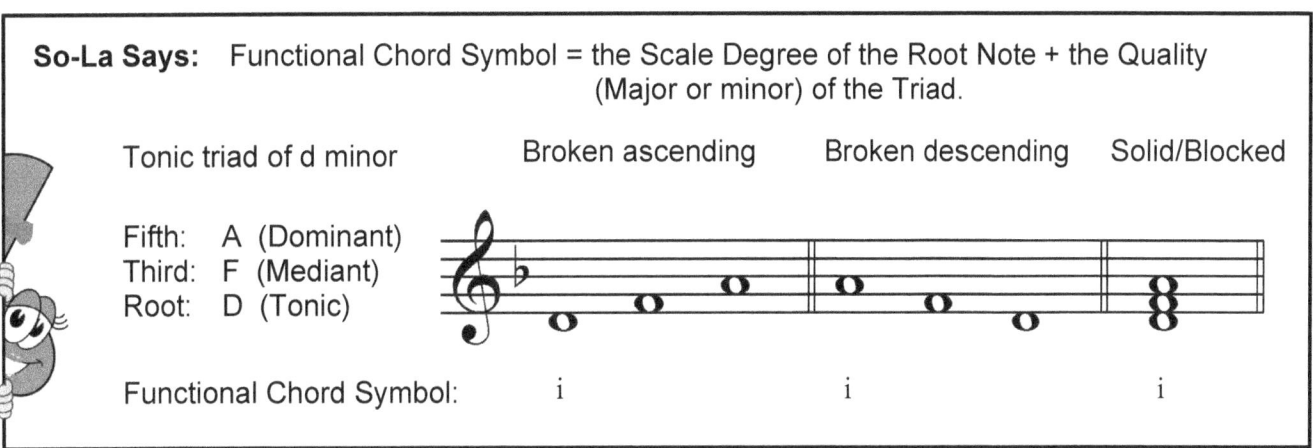

So-La Says: Functional Chord Symbol = the Scale Degree of the Root Note + the Quality
(Major or minor) of the Triad.

Tonic triad of d minor   Broken ascending   Broken descending   Solid/Blocked

Fifth: A (Dominant)
Third: F (Mediant)
Root: D (Tonic)

Functional Chord Symbol: i   i   i

1. For each of the following minor key Tonic triads:
   a) Name the Third (Mediant) and the Fifth (Dominant) above the Root (Tonic).
   b) In Measure 1, write the notes of the broken ascending Tonic triad. Use whole notes.
   c) In Measure 2, write the notes of the broken descending Tonic triad. Use whole notes.
   d) In Measure 3, write the notes of the solid/blocked Tonic triad. Use whole notes.

Tonic triad of e minor   Broken ascending   Broken descending   Solid/Blocked

Fifth: _____

Third: _____

Root: __E__

Functional Chord Symbol: i   i   i

Tonic triad of a minor   Broken ascending   Broken descending   Solid/Blocked

Fifth: _____

Third: _____

Root: __A__

Functional Chord Symbol: i   i   i

♩ **Ti-Do Time:**   LISTEN as your Teacher plays the minor Tonic triads in Exercise 1.
Identify the triad as broken ascending, broken descending or solid.

TRIAD QUALITY - MAJOR and MINOR (Use after Prep 2 Rudiments Page 104)

A Triad contains a Root, a Third and a Fifth. When the distance between the Root and the Third of the triad is 4 half steps (semitones), the quality of the triad is **Major**.

When the distance between the Root and the Third of the triad is 3 half steps (semitones), the quality of the triad is **minor**. The interval of a minor Third is one half step smaller than a Major Third.

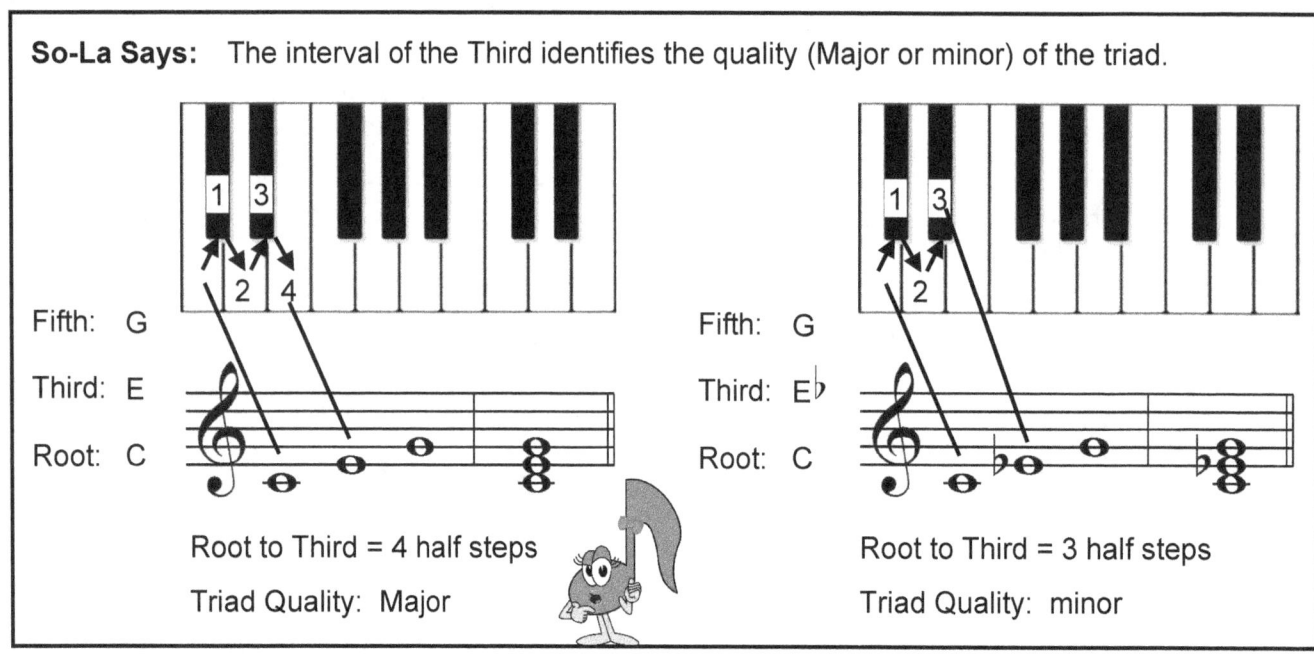

1. For each of the following:
   a) Name the letter names for the Root, Third and Fifth.
   b) In Measure 1, draw a line from the Root and the Third notes on the staff to the corresponding keys on the keyboard. Identify the Root to Third as 4 half steps or as 3 half steps.
   c) Identify the Triad Quality as Major or minor.

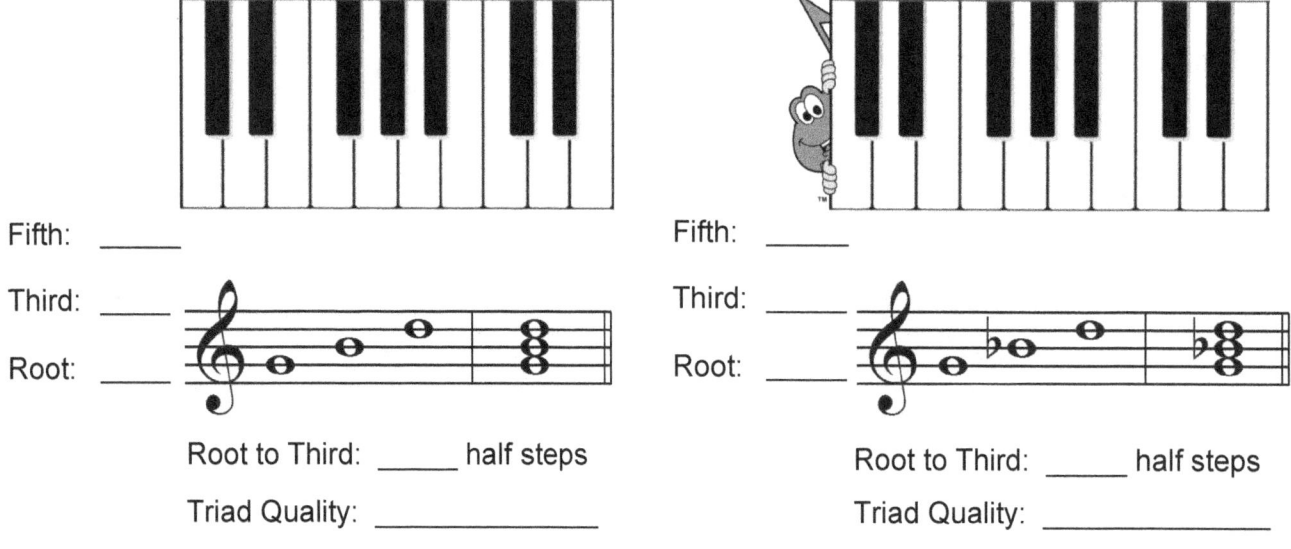

♪ **Ti-Do Time:** PLAY the Major and minor triads in the Example Box and in Exercise 1.
LISTEN. Can you hear the difference between a Major and a minor triad?

ROOT/QUALITY CHORD SYMBOLS (Use after Prep 2 Rudiments Page 104)

Root/Quality Chord Symbols are Letter Names that indicate the quality (Major or minor) of a triad.

An Upper Case letter indicates a Major triad. (Example: C)
An Upper Case letter with an "m" after it indicates a minor triad. (Example: Cm)

So-La Says: The Root/Quality Chord Symbol is written above the first note of the triad.

Root/Quality Chord Symbol: D   D   D

Root/Quality Chord Symbol: Dm   Dm   Dm

Root (D) to Third (F#) = 4 half steps
Triad Quality: Major

Root (D) to Third (F) = 3 half steps
Triad Quality: minor

♫ **Ti-Do Tip:** Letter names are written with an Upper Case (Capital) letter. An Upper Case letter is used to identify the Root in the Root/Quality Chord Symbol as the Root is a letter name.

1. For each of the following:
    a) Name the letter names for the Root and Third.
    b) Identify the Root to Third as 4 half steps or as 3 half steps.
    c) Identify the Triad Quality as Major or minor.
    d) Write the Root/Quality Chord Symbol above the first note of each triad.

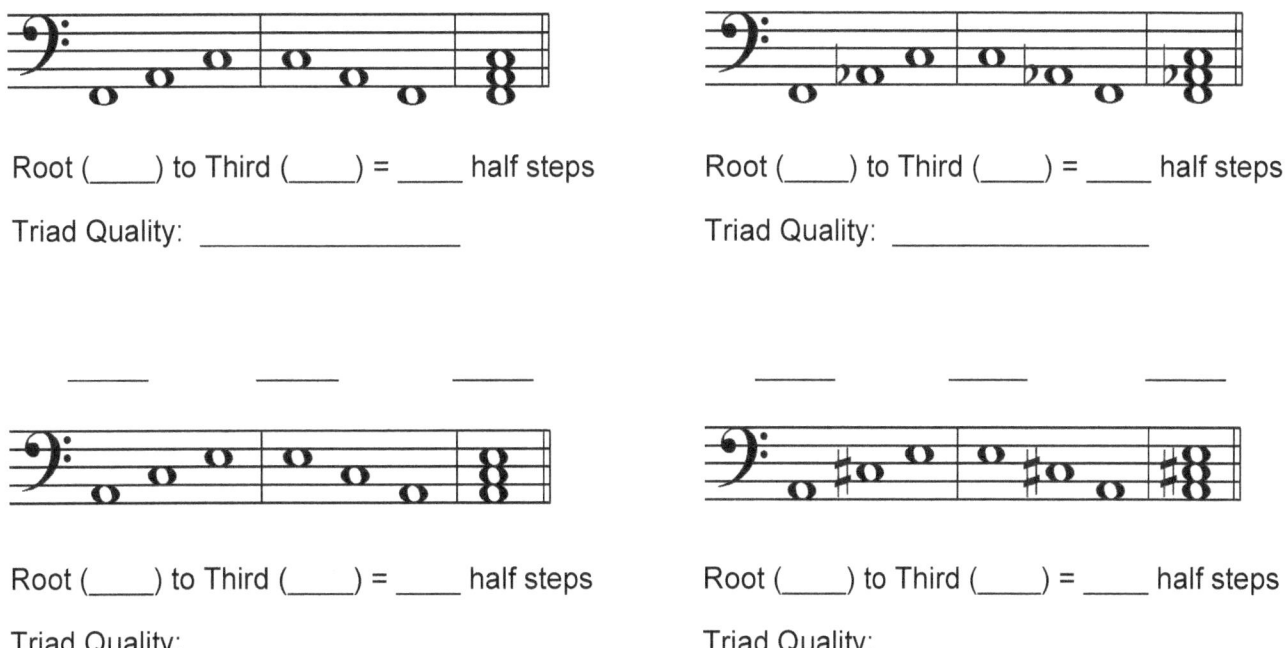

Root (____) to Third (____) = ____ half steps
Triad Quality: _____

Root (____) to Third (____) = ____ half steps
Triad Quality: _____

Root (____) to Third (____) = ____ half steps
Triad Quality: _____

Root (____) to Third (____) = ____ half steps
Triad Quality: _____

FUNCTIONAL CHORD SYMBOLS and ROOT/QUALITY CHORD SYMBOLS - MAJOR SCALES
(Use after Prep 2 Rudiments Page 111)

The Triad built on the Tonic ($\hat{1}$) of the Major scale is always a **Major triad**, I (a happy sound).

The **Functional Chord Symbol** (Roman Numeral) of the triad built on the Tonic of the Major scale is I.

The **Root/Quality Chord Symbol** of the triad built on the Tonic of the Major scale is a Major quality.

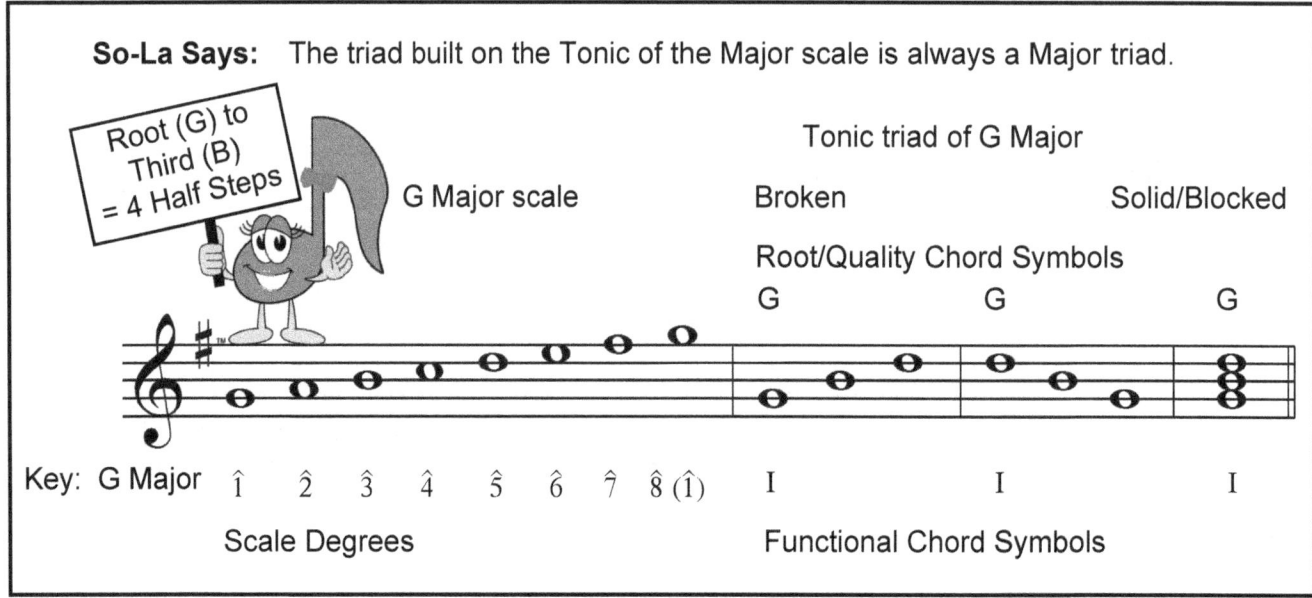

♫ **Ti-Do Tip:** In a Major triad, the distance from the Root to the Third is always 4 half steps.

1. a) Write the Scale Degree Numbers below the notes of the F Major scale.
   b) Write the Functional Chord Symbol of each F Major Tonic triad below the staff.
   c) Write the Root/Quality Chord Symbol of each F Major triad above the staff.

♫ **Ti-Do Time:** Your Teacher will PLAY the Major Tonic triads in the Example and in the Exercise. LISTEN. Identify the triad as broken ascending, broken descending or solid.

FUNCTIONAL CHORD SYMBOLS and ROOT/QUALITY CHORD SYMBOLS - MINOR SCALES
(Use after Prep 2 Rudiments Page 111)

The Triad built on the Tonic ($\hat{1}$) of the minor scale is always a **minor triad**, i (a sad sound).

The **Functional Chord Symbol** (Roman Numeral) of the triad built on the Tonic of the minor scale is i.

The **Root/Quality Chord Symbol** of the triad built on the Tonic of the minor scale is a minor quality.

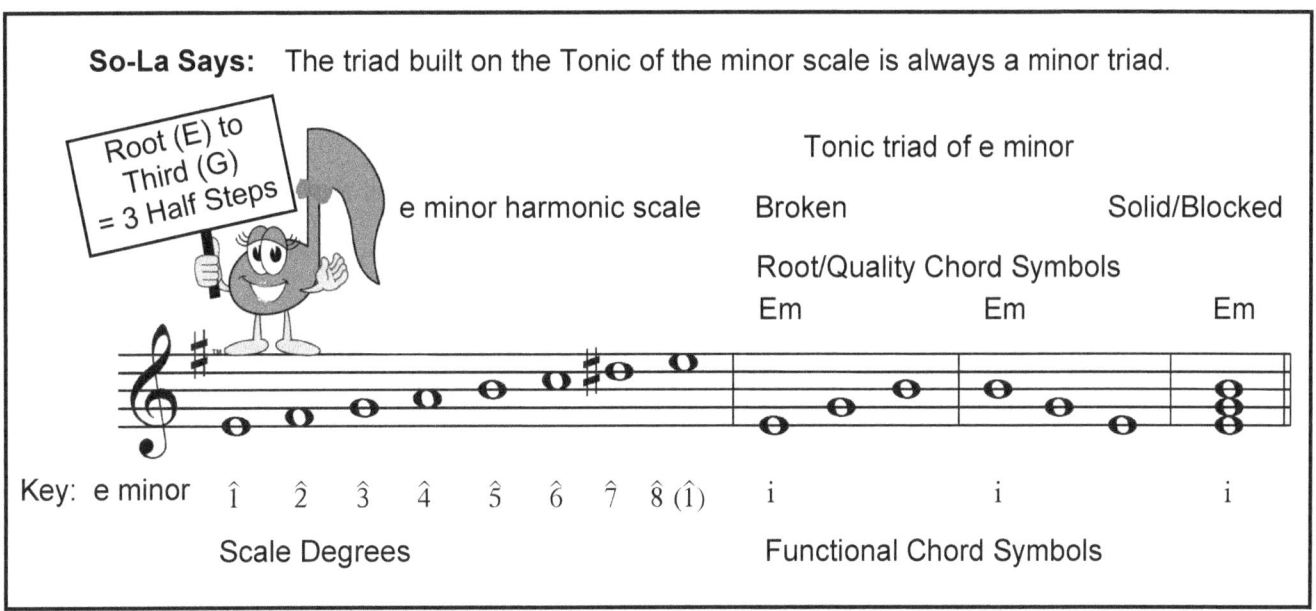

♫ **Ti-Do Tip:** In a minor triad, the distance from the Root to the Third is always 3 half steps.

1. a) Write the Scale Degree Numbers below the notes of the d minor harmonic scale.
   b) Write the Functional Chord Symbol of each d minor Tonic triad below the staff.
   c) Write the Root/Quality Chord Symbol of each d minor triad above the staff.

♫ **Ti-Do Time:** Your Teacher will PLAY the minor Tonic triads in the Example and in the Exercise.
LISTEN. Identify the triad as broken ascending, broken descending or solid.

FUNCTIONAL CHORD SYMBOLS and ROOT/QUALITY CHORD SYMBOLS - MAJOR or MINOR
(Use after Prep 2 Rudiments Page 111)

The **Major** Tonic triad belongs to the Major key of the Tonic note.

The **minor** Tonic triad belongs to the minor key of the Tonic note.

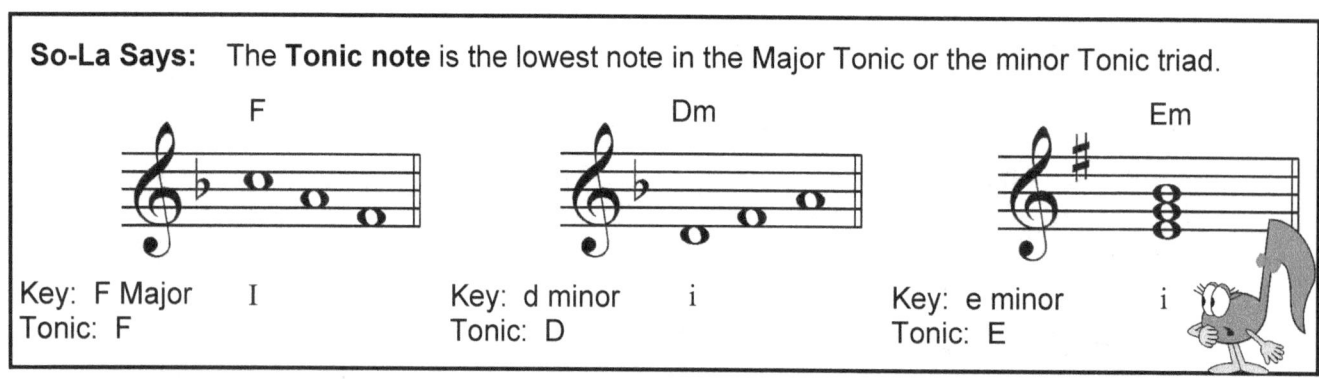

♫ **Ti-Do Tip:** The Tonic note in a Tonic triad (in Root Position) is always the lowest note. The Tonic note is the first note in an ascending triad and the last note in a descending triad.

1. For each Tonic triad:
   a) Name the Tonic Note and the Major or minor key.
   b) Write the Functional Chord Symbol below the staff.
   c) Write the Root/Quality Chord Symbol above the staff.

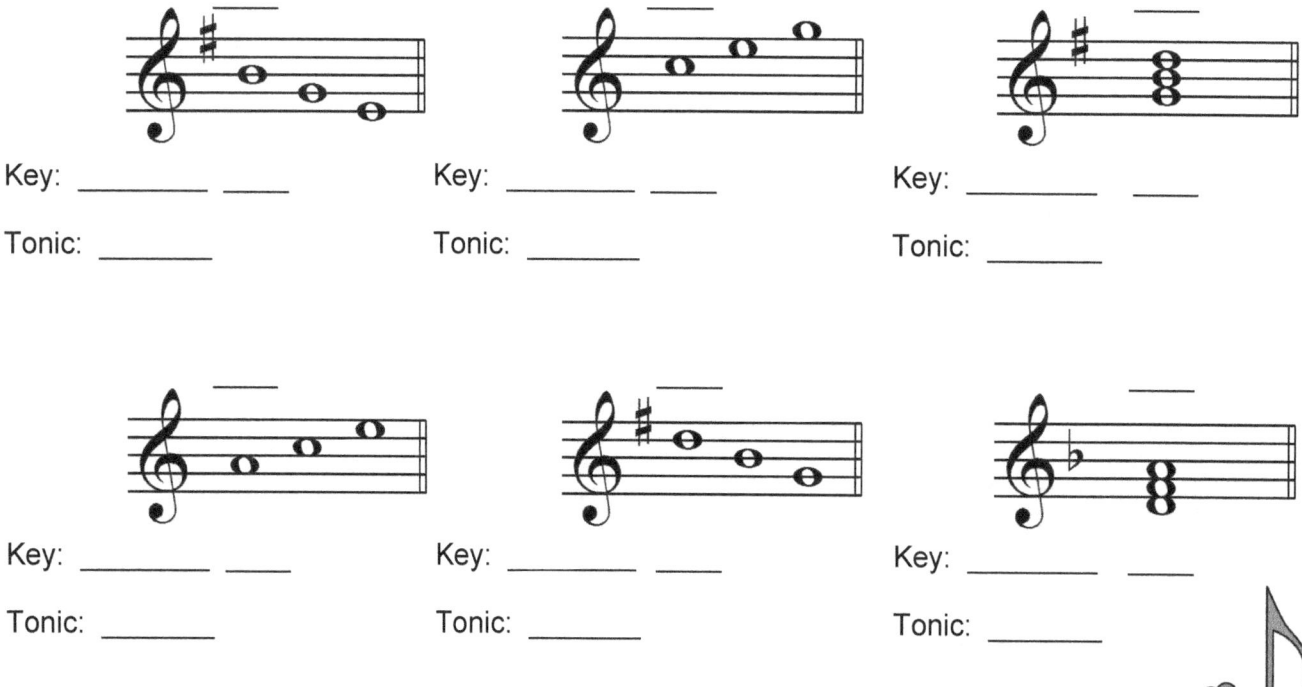

♫ **Ti-Do Time:** Your Teacher will PLAY the triads in the Example and in the Exercise. LISTEN. Identify the triad as a Major triad or as a minor triad.

MUSIC TERMS and SIGNS - D.C. al Fine and REPEAT SIGNS (Use after Page 117)

A **Repeat** sign is written as two **dots** (one in space 2 and one in space 3) in front of a double bar line (one thin bar line and one thick bar line).

A **Repeat sign** indicates that the music is repeated from the beginning of the piece.

When there are **two** repeat signs, the music is repeated within the double bar lines.

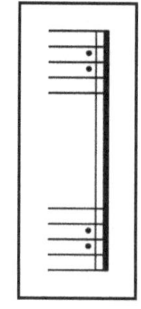

1. Play the melody below on your instrument. Analyze the music by answering the questions below.

a) Name the Major key. _____ Name the Tonic note. _____

b) How many measures are written in the melody above? _____

c) When all repeat signs are followed, how many measures are played? _____

So-La Says: Other Musical Terms can be used to repeat larger sections of music!

da capo, **D.C.** means repeat from the beginning.

dal segno, **D.S.** means repeat from the sign (𝄋).

Fine means "the end" of the piece of music.

D.C. al Fine means repeat from the beginning and end at the word *Fine*.

D.S. al Fine means repeat from the sign (𝄋) and end at the word *Fine*.

---

2. Draw a line to match the Musical Term or Sign with the correct definition.

𝄋	The end of the piece.
D.C.	Repeat from the beginning.
D.S.	Repeat from the sign (𝄋).
Fine	Repeat from the sign and end at the word *Fine*.
D.S. al Fine	Repeat from the beginning and end at the word *Fine*.
D.C. al Fine	The "sign" used to indicate where to repeat in a *D.S. al Fine*.

MUSIC TERMS and SIGNS (Use after Prep 2 Rudiments Page 117)

Musical Terms provide descriptions as to how the Composer would like their piece performed.

Musical Term	Definition
molto	much, very
poco	little
rallentando (rall.)	slowing down

So-La Says: Musical Terms like "***molto***" and "***poco***" are a prefix (a word that comes before another) used to enhance musical descriptions.

Example: *molto rallentando* = slowing down very much

poco rallentando = slowing down a little

♪ **Ti-Do Tip:** "***Ritardano***" (rit.) and "***Rallentando***" (rall.) both indicate to slow the tempo down.

1. Fill in the blank with the correct Musical Term.

   a) _____ is a musical term meaning "little".

   b) _____ is a musical term meaning "much, very".

So-La Says: On the piano, **PEDALS** change the tone quality.

LEFT PEDAL	MIDDLE PEDAL	RIGHT PEDAL
una corda or **una corde pedal** softens (or mellows) the tone (played with the left foot)	**sostenuto pedal** sustains any notes that are held down when the pedal is depressed	**damper** or **sustain pedal** prolongs and connects tones (played with the right foot)

The middle "**sostenuto**" pedal is not found on all pianos. It may also have a different function.

Con pedale, ***con ped***. or the sign 𝄢 indicate to use the damper pedal.
Other markings used to indicate the use of the damper pedal are ⌊___∧___⌋ and ⌊_____⌋.

2. Label the 3 pedals as una corda, sostenuto or damper pedal.

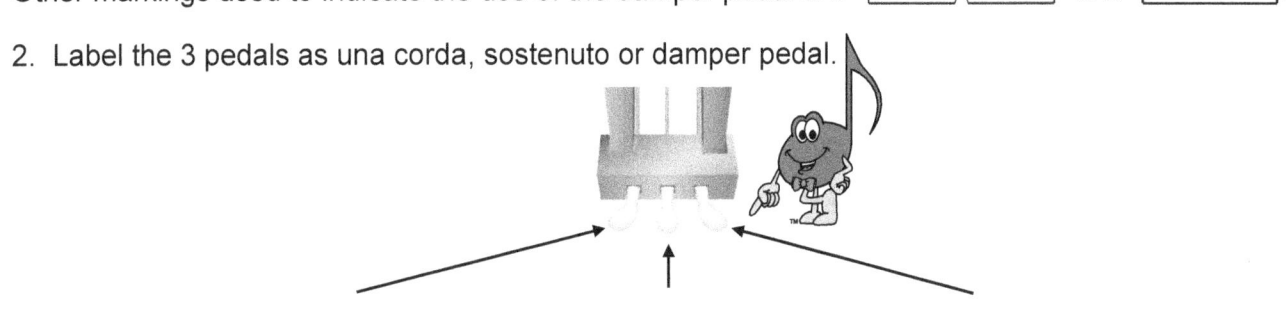

MELODY WRITING - ENDING on SCALE DEGREE 1̂ (Use after Prep 2 Rudiments Page 117)

A melody may be based on the notes of a Major Scale. A melody that ends on the Tonic note (stable degree 1̂) sounds finished, like a period (musical period) at the end of a sentence.

1. This melody is in the key of G Major and ends on the Tonic note (stable degree 1̂). Play the melody on your instrument. Listen for the motive and repeated patterns.

   a) The melody is in the key of ___ Major and ends on the _____ note (stable degree ___).

   b) Circle if the motive in measure 1 is repeated in measure 2 as: rhythmic   or   melodic/rhythmic.

   c) Circle if the melodic pattern in measure 2 and in measure 3 are the: same   or   different.

   d) The melody ends on the Tonic note _____. The Tonic note is played _____ times.

♫ **Ti-Do Tip:** A melody may use notes that move by step, skip or repeated notes. A melody written in a Major key may end on the Tonic note (stable degree 1̂) of the Major scale.

2. Compose two melodies (G Major and F Major). Use repeated notes and notes moving by step or skip. Use the given rhythm. End on the stable degree (1̂). Draw a double bar line at the end.

Key: _____ Major   Tonic Stable Degree: _____

Key: _____ Major   Tonic Stable Degree: _____

MELODY WRITING - ENDING on SCALE DEGREE $\hat{3}$ (Use after Prep 2 Rudiments Page 117)

A melody (or musical sentence) ends on a stable degree (or musical period) so it sounds finished. A melody may end on the Tonic note (stable degree $\hat{1}$) OR end on the Mediant note (stable degree $\hat{3}$).

1. This melody is in the key of F Major and ends on the Mediant note A (stable degree $\hat{3}$). Play the melody on your instrument. Listen for the motive and repeated patterns.

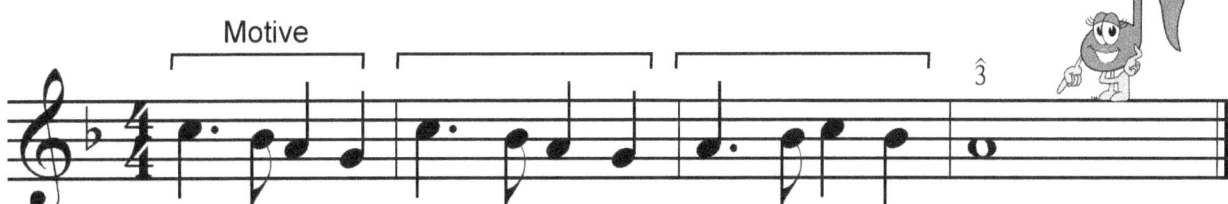

   a) The melody is in the key of ___ Major and ends on the _____ note (stable degree ___).

   b) Circle if the motive in measure 1 is repeated in measure 2 as: rhythmic or melodic/rhythmic.

   c) Circle if the melodic pattern in measure 2 and in measure 3 are the: same or different.

   d) The melody ends on the Mediant note _____. The Mediant note is played _____ times.

♫ **Ti-Do Tip:** When composing a melody, first sing or play your melodic idea using the given rhythm. Explore interval patterns. End on the Mediant note (stable degree $\hat{3}$) of the Major scale.

2. Compose two melodies (F Major and G Major). Use repeated notes and notes moving by step or skip. Use the given rhythm. End on the stable degree ($\hat{3}$). Draw a double bar line at the end.

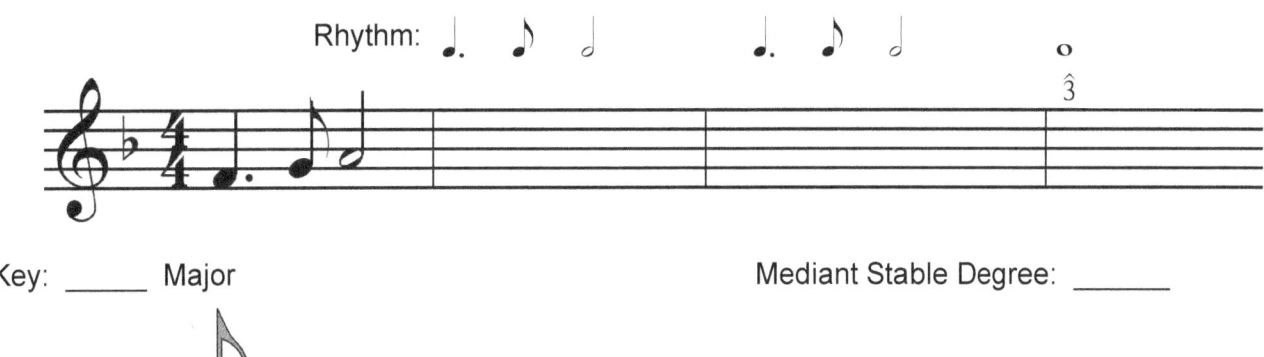

Key: _____ Major   Mediant Stable Degree: _____

Key: _____ Major   Mediant Stable Degree: _____

UltimateMusicTheory.com © Copyright 2017 Gloryland Publishing. All Rights Reserved.

MELODY - PHRASE ENDING on UNSTABLE OR STABLE SCALE DEGREES
(Use after Prep 2 Rudiments Page 117)

A melody has a motive (short melodic or rhythmic pattern) which may be repeated in a phrase. A phrase is composed of several motives and is a single musical idea (or musical sentence).

♫ **Ti-Do Tip:** A phrase may be indicated by a slur (a curved line) above or below the notes. A phrase within a melody may end on an unstable scale degree ($\hat{2}$ or $\hat{7}$). A phrase at the end of a melody may end on a stable degree ($\hat{1}$ or $\hat{3}$).

1. Copy the C Major scale. Write the scale degrees below each note.

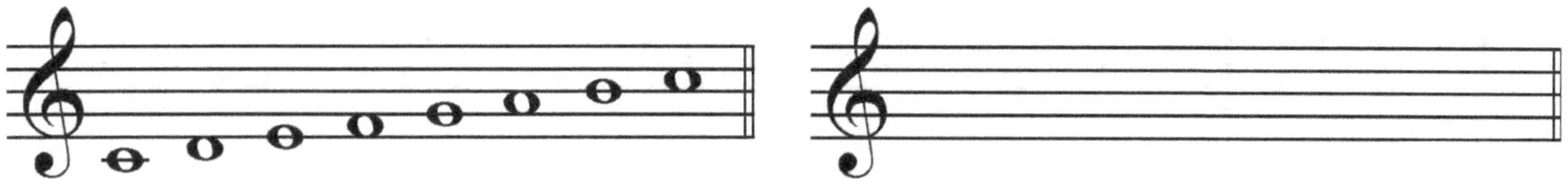

$\hat{1}$ $\hat{2}$ $\hat{3}$ $\hat{4}$ $\hat{5}$ $\hat{6}$ $\hat{7}$ $\hat{8}$ ($\hat{1}$) ___ ___ ___ ___ ___ ___ ___ ___

2. For each melody, name the Major key. Identify the scale degree at the end of each phrase as an unstable scale degree ($\hat{2}$ or $\hat{7}$) OR stable scale degree ($\hat{1}$ or $\hat{3}$). Sing or play each melody.

____________ scale degree: _____

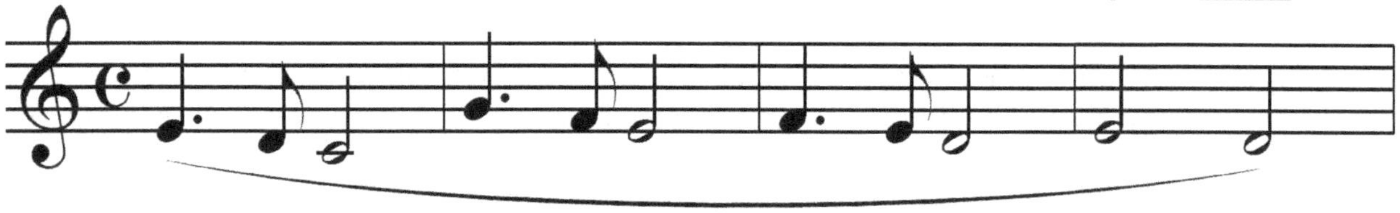

Key: _____ Major

____________ scale degree: _____

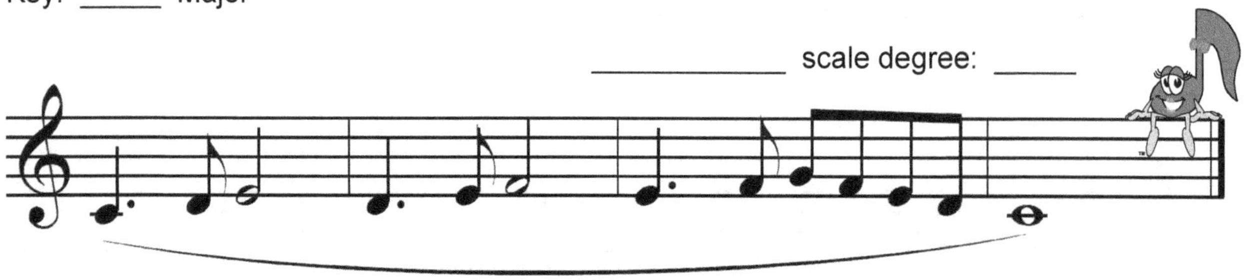

____________ scale degree: _____ ____________ scale degree: _____

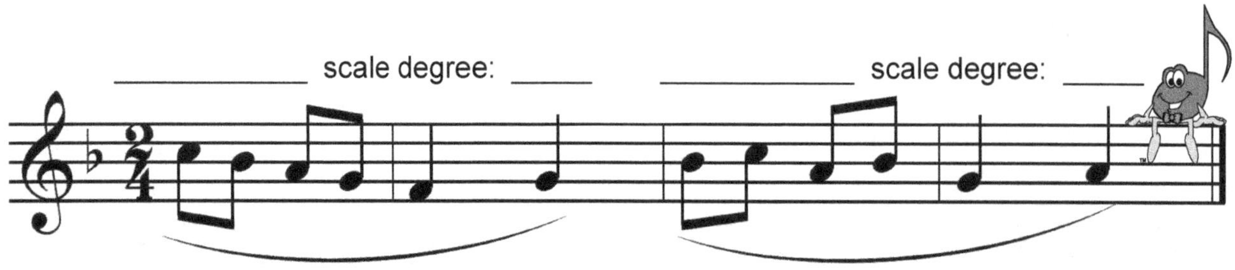

Key: _____ Major

MELODY WRITING - PHRASE ENDING on a STABLE SCALE DEGREES
(Use after Prep 2 Rudiments Page 117)

A melody may have a repeated pattern that uses the same intervals (melodic pattern) and the same note values (rhythmic pattern). A repeated pattern can start at the same pitch or at a different pitch.

Repetition: A melodic/rhythmic pattern repeated at the identical (same) pitch.

Sequence: A melodic/rhythmic pattern repeated at a higher or lower pitch.

♫ **Ti-Do Tip:** A phrase will not be indicated by a slur when the articulation is to be played detached.

IMAGINE, COMPOSE, EXPLORE (Use after Prep 2 Rudiments Page 117)

Composing, or melody writing, means to create new music. After you compose your music, sing or play your composition on your instrument.

♪ **I**magine the music telling a story or idea. The title (written at the top) describes the composition.
♪ **C**ompose your musical idea. The name (written at the top right) identifies the composer.
♪ **E**xplore the music. Add "So-La Sparkles" using dynamics and articulation to enhance the sound.

So-La Says: First compose freely without writing anything down. Use a recording device to record yourself. Use the recording to assist you in writing out your composition.

♫ **Ti-Do Tip:** Always add a double bar line at the end of your melody.

1. For each of the following: compose a melody in measures 2, 3 & 4. Use the given rhythm.

    a) Imagine your musical idea by completing the title at the top. Write your name as the composer.
    b) Compose a melody using repeated notes, steps or skips. End on stable scale degree $\hat{1}$ or $\hat{3}$.
    c) Explore the music. Add "So-La Sparkles" using dynamics and articulation. Play your piece.

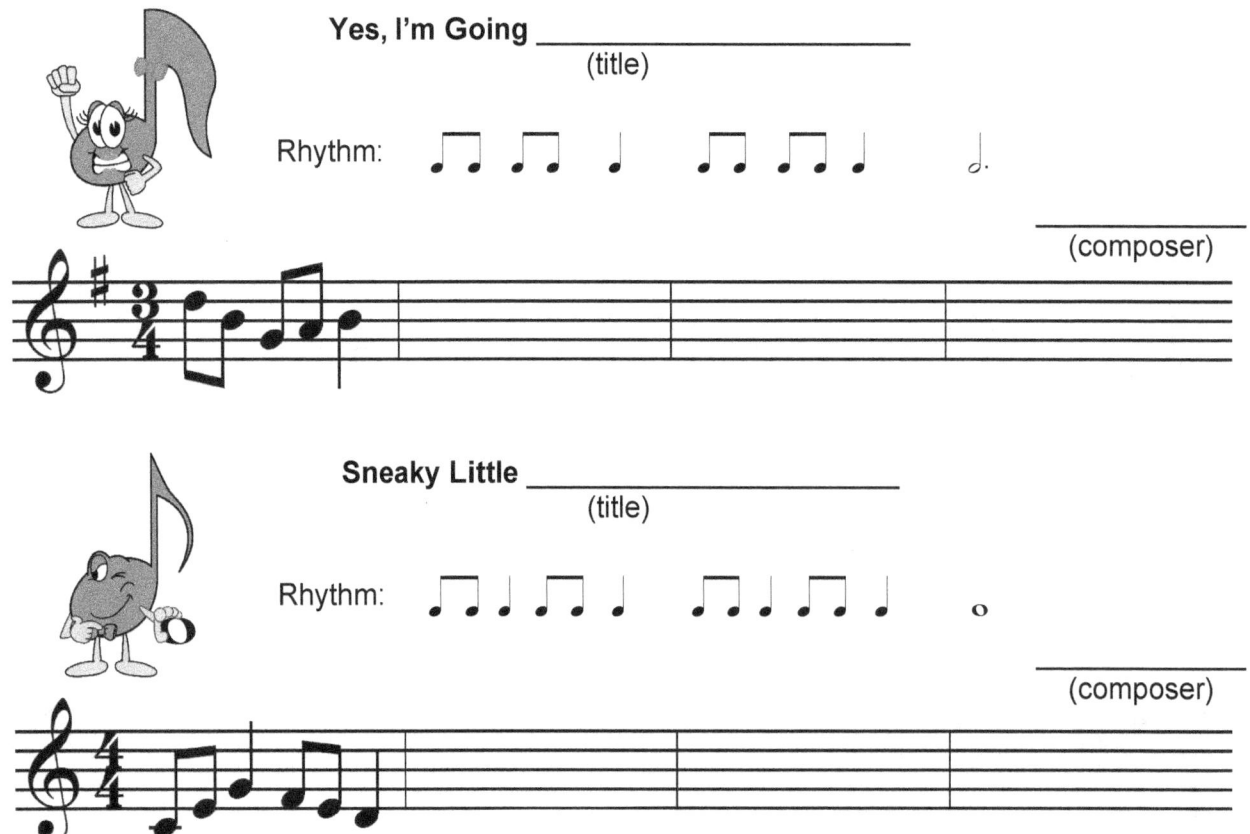

ANALYSIS, MUSICAL TERMS and SIGHT READING (Use after Prep 2 Rudiments Page 117)

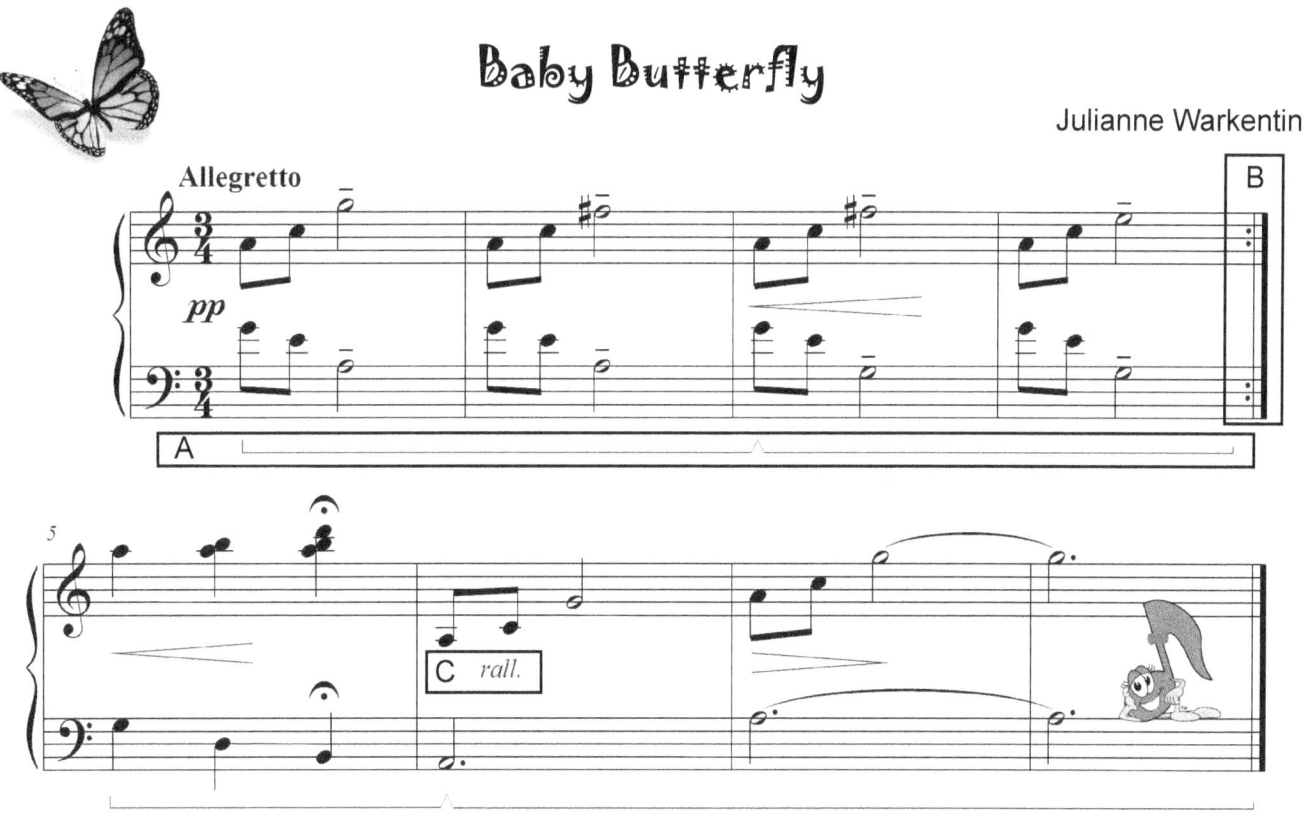

1. Analyze the piece of music by answering the questions below.

   a) Name and explain the Tempo. _____

   b) Is the rhythmic pattern of the motive in measure 1 repeated in measure 2? _____

   c) Explain the sign at the letter A. _____

   d) Explain the sign at the letter B. _____

   e) Explain the term at the letter C. _____

 ♫ **Ti-Do Time:** IDENTIFY the Time Signature.

TAP a steady Basic Beat with your foot. CLAP the rhythm in the Treble Clef. Count out loud.

So-La Says: PLAY (Sight Read) the "Baby Butterfly". Observe all the Musical Terms and Signs. Remember to use the pedal.

MUSIC HISTORY - WOLFGANG AMADEUS MOZART (1756 - 1791)

Wolfgang Amadeus Mozart was born in 1756 in Salzburg, Austria. His father was Leopold Mozart, a violinist in the orchestra of the Archbishop of Salzburg. He was a famous teacher and composer.

When he was 4 years old, young Wolfgang started music lessons with his father.

He composed his first piece when he was 5!

By the age of 6, the young Mozart could play the harpsichord, organ and violin!

At the age of 8, he wrote his first Symphony (No. 1 in E flat Major, K. 16).

He wrote his first Opera (Apollo et Hyacinthus) when he was 11.

Mozart visited and performed in Vienna, Austria (1762); Paris, France (1763); London, England (1764) and Italy (1769). They traveled across Europe by stagecoach (horse-drawn carriages).

Since these tours took months to complete, Mozart didn't go to school. He learned from his father, from tutors and from the musicians that he met on his travels.

Mozart had an older sister, Maria Anna, whose nickname was "Nannerl". Young Wolfgang loved to watch his father give his sister music lessons.

Everyone was impressed with how well Mozart could improvise and compose on the piano and the violin.

Mozart could also sight read and play anything perfectly the first time he saw it.

In 1782, Mozart married Constanze. Their son Franz Xaver (Wolfgang Amadeus Mozart, Jr.) was the youngest child of six, and the only one to make music his career.

On November 22, 1791, while living in Vienna (the Capital City of Austria), Mozart became ill with a very high fever. He died on December 5, 1791. He was only 35 years old.

1. Check (✓) the correct answer.

   a) How old was Mozart when he started music lessons? ☐ 4 years old or ☐ 6 years old

   b) How old was he when he wrote his first opera? ☐ 8 years old or ☐ 11 years old

   c) How old was Mozart when he died? ☐ 35 years old or ☐ 50 years old

MUSIC HISTORY - WOLFGANG AMADEUS MOZART - MUSIC (SYMPHONY and OPERA)

Mozart wrote over 600 compositions, including symphonies, operas, sonatas and concertos.

While in England, Mozart studied the music of Johann Christian Bach, the youngest son of Johann Sebastian Bach. The singing melodies of Johann Christian Bach's music inspired Mozart to start writing Symphonies.

> A **Symphony** is a work (piece of music) for an Orchestra. It usually has 3 or 4 separate movements. These movements can also be performed separately.
>
> It is important to listen to all the movements of the Symphony in order to understand what the Composer is saying in the music.

Mozart composed at least 41 symphonies. One of his most famous was Symphony No. 40 Eine Kleine Nachtmusik (A Little Night Music, 1787).

1. Fill in the blanks.

   a) A Symphony is a piece of music written for an _____.

   b) Mozart composed at least _____ symphonies. He composed his first symphony at age _____.

> An **Opera** combines singing, acting, scenery and music (played by an Orchestra) into a dramatic presentation that tells a story.
>
> The text of an opera (the words that are sung or sometimes spoken) is called the **Libretto**. The libretto is the story line of the opera.

Mozart's favorite music to write was Opera. He also wrote for piano, voice, orchestras and chamber groups (small groups of instruments).

At the age of 14, he conducted his opera "Mithridates, King of Pontus" for 20 performances.

Mozart composed numerous Operas including "The Marriage of Figaro" and "The Magic Flute".

2. Fill in the blanks.

   a) An Opera is a dramatic presentation that tells a _____.

   b) The name of one of Mozart's Operas is _____.

MUSIC HISTORY - TWELVE VARIATIONS on AH, VOUS DIRAI-JE, MAMAN, K265

Music written in a "**Theme and Variations**" form has been popular for hundreds of years.

When Mozart was 22 years old (in 1778), he wrote a "Theme and Variations" piece based on the popular nursery rhyme Twinkle, Twinkle, Little Star. It was called "Ah, vous dirai-je, Maman, K 265".

> The letter "**K**", found at the end of the title of each of Mozart's Compositions, is the initial of Dr. Ludwig von Köchel. Dr. Köchel was an Austrian botanist who published a catalogue of Mozart's Compositions. The Compositions are numbered in the approximate order that they were written.

In a "Theme and Variations", a theme is played by the instrument (or instruments). It is then repeated (the "Variations") with changes in melody, harmony, rhythm and/or texture (number of voices heard).

Go to **GSGMUSIC.com** - For Easy Access to music for listening to Ah, vous dirai-je, Maman, K 265.

1. Listen to Mozart's - 12 Variations in C Major ($\frac{2}{4}$ Time) Ah vous dirai-je, Maman, K 265. Observe the changes to the theme (melody, rhythm, accompaniment, articulation, tempo, tonality and Time Signature). Check (✓) the correct answer to the questions below.

Theme: The melody is introduced in the right hand with simple accompaniment in the left hand. In each Variation a change occurs to the theme. The change to the theme is when:

Variation 1: The melody (played in the right hand) is embellished as the rhythm is played:

☐ Fast running sixteenth notes ☐ Slow walking half notes

Variation 2: The accompaniment (played in the left hand) is embellished as the rhythm is played:

☐ Slow walking half notes ☐ Fast running sixteenth notes

Variation 3: The melody is embellished as the rhythm and articulation are played:

☐ Dotted half notes and pedal ☐ Triplet notes and staccatos

Variation 4: The accompaniment is embellished as the rhythm and articulation are played:

☐ Triplet notes and staccatos ☐ Dotted half notes and pedal

MUSIC HISTORY - AH, VOUS DIRAI-JE, MAMAN, K265 - TWINKLE, TWINKLE, LITTLE STAR

Variation 5: The melody is embellished as the pulse of the rhythm is played:

☐ On the Basic Beat patterns ☐ Off the Basic Beat patterns

Variation 6: The melody (played in the right hand) is embellished as the theme is played with:

☐ Chords ☐ Single notes

Variation 7: The melody (played in the right hand) is embellished as the rhythm is played:

☐ Slow long tied notes ☐ Fast running scale patterns

Variation 8: The melody is presented in c minor (change in tonality) and is played with:

☐ Imitation between right & left hand ☐ Left hand only

Variation 9: The melody is embellished as the articulation is played:

☐ Legato ☐ Staccato

Variation 10: The accompaniment is embellished with sixteenth notes as the melody is played with:

☐ The left hand ☐ The right hand

Variation 11: The melody is embellished as the tempo and style are played:

☐ Allegro and in a Marching Style ☐ Adagio and in a Singing Style

Variation 12: The melody is embellished as the tempo and Time Signature are changed to:

☐ Allegro and $\frac{3}{4}$ Time Signature ☐ Adagio and $\frac{4}{4}$ Time Signature

MUSIC HISTORY - CONCERTO

A **Concerto** is a piece of music that features a soloist (or smaller solo group of instruments) performing with an Orchestra (a larger group of performers).

The "**Concerto**" gets its name from an Italian word that means "to compete, or strive against".

> A **Concerto** could be written for:
> ♪ a soloist (one person playing one instrument) playing "against" an orchestra;
> ♪ a small group of instruments playing "against" a larger group of instruments;
> ♪ one instrumental family playing "against" the other instrumental families of the orchestra.

A Concerto is a special type of piece that will "pit" the solo instrument (or instruments) against the larger orchestral group.

> Mozart wrote Concertos for the Piano, French Horn, Violin and other instruments of the Orchestra. His list of Concertos includes:
>
>  25 Concertos for one or more Pianos and Orchestra. Mozart's favorite instrument was the Piano. He loved to play and write music for the piano.
>
>  5 Concertos for Violin and Orchestra.
>
>  4 Concertos for French Horn and Orchestra. When he died, he left 2 unfinished Concertos for French Horn and Orchestra.

It is fun to listen to how the soloist (the solo group) will have the theme, and then the orchestra (the large group) will "take" the theme and play with it until the soloist takes it back.

The Concerto has been popular for over 250 years! Composers would write the Concerto as a way to challenge the soloist and instrumentalists to play to the very best of their abilities.

1. Fill in the blanks.

    a) A Concerto could have one soloist playing against an _____.

    b) The Concerto has been a popular form of music for over _____ years.

    c) Mozart's favorite instrument was the _____.

MUSIC HISTORY - RONDO FORM

A Concerto has **3 Movements**.

A **Movement** is a section of the music that is complete all by itself. Each Movement can be performed as an individual piece of music. Each Movement of the Concerto will have a different Tempo (rate of speed) and will usually have it's own unique theme or motive.

The First Movement of a Concerto is often *Allegro* - to be performed at a fast, lively, "bustling" tempo.

The Second Movement of a Concerto is often *Lento* - to be performed songlike and slow.

The Third Movement of a Concerto is often *Allegro* - at an upbeat and spirited tempo with a rousing finish (but in a different Key Signature from the First Movement).

Mozart often wrote the Third Movement of the Concerto in "**Rondo Form**".

1. Add the correct Tempo for each Movement of a Concerto.

    a) The First Movement of a Concerto is often performed _____.

    b) The Second Movement of a Concerto is often performed _____.

    c) The Third Movement of a Concerto is often performed _____.

Rondo Form is one of the most important musical forms. In Rondo Form, a single main theme will alternate with new musical ideas (called "Episodes") brought in as the piece of music develops.

The main Rondo theme is identified as "Theme **A**".

When analyzing the form of a Rondo, each new idea (or Episode) has its own letter of the alphabet.

The form of a Rondo might look like this:
   A - B - A - C - A   or   A - B - A - C - A - D - A   or   A - B - A - C - A - B - A

2. Fill in the blanks.

    a) Mozart often wrote the Third Movement of the Concerto in _____ Form.

    b) The main theme of a Rondo is identified as Theme _____.

    c) Each new musical idea in a Rondo is called an _____.

MUSIC HISTORY - HORN CONCERTO No. 4 in E flat Major, K 495, THIRD MOVEMENT, RONDO

The Horn Concerto No. 4 in E flat Major, K 495 by Wolfgang Amadeus Mozart features the Third Movement in Rondo Form.

The Rondo theme is a 4 measure phrase. This main Rondo theme is identified as "Theme **A**".

Go to **GSGMUSIC.com** - For Easy Access to music for listening to Horn Concerto No. 4, K 495.

1. Listen to Mozart's - Horn Concerto No. 4 in E flat Major, K 495 - Third Movement in Rondo Form. Observe the Rondo Form A B A C A. The Rondo Theme A is introduced at the beginning of the music. Check (✓) the correct answer to the questions below.

Theme: The Rondo Theme is presented by the French Horn (solo) and the Orchestra. Listen as they compete or "challenge" each other in the Rondo Theme. The Rondo Theme is Theme A.

a) Theme A (The Rondo Theme) is first introduced at the beginning of the music by the:

☐ French Horn ☐ Orchestra

b) Theme A is repeated (played again) by the:

☐ French Horn ☐ Orchestra

c) When Theme A is played between Theme B and Theme C, it is played (repeated):

☐ Three times ☐ Seven times

d) The tempo of Theme A, heard in the Third Movement of the Horn Concerto, is:

☐ Allegro ☐ Adagio

TAP with TI-DO in 2/4 TIME

A **Time Signature** has two numbers and is written on the staff after the clef.

The **TOP** number **2**, **3** or **4** indicates the number of beats per measure.

The **BOTTOM** number **4** indicates **one quarter note** (♩) is equal to **ONE** Basic Beat.

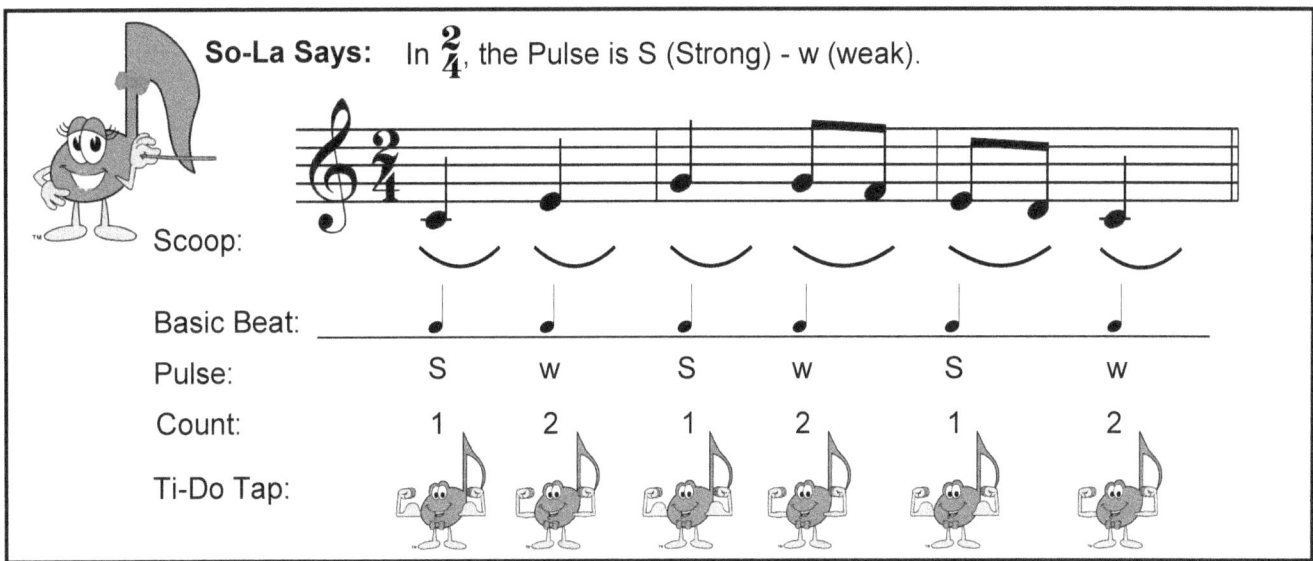

♫ **Ti-Do Tip:** The **PULSE** is where the rhythmic emphasis falls in a measure.
UPPER case letter for **S** (Strong) and lower case letter for **w** (weak).

1. Following the Example:
   a) Scoop each Basic Beat in each measure.
   b) Write the Basic Beat below the Scoop.
   c) Write the Pulse below each Basic Beat.
   d) Write the Counts below each Pulse.

♫ **Ti-Do Time:** TAP the Basic Beat with your foot while you CLAP each rhythm.
COUNT out loud while you TAP and CLAP.

TAP with TI-DO in 3/4 TIME

In $\frac{3}{4}$ Time, there are 3 quarter note Basic Beats (3 counts) in each measure.

1. Add bar lines to complete this rhythm in $\frac{3}{4}$.

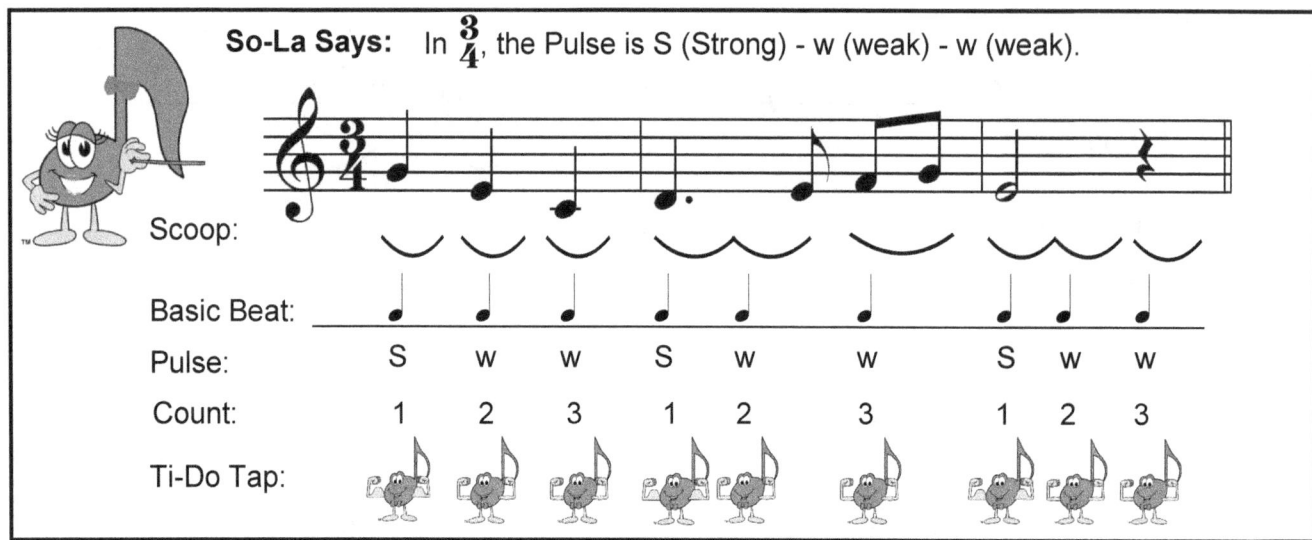

♪ **Ti-Do Tip:** UPPER case letter for **S** (Strong) and lower case letter for **w** (weak).

2. Following the Example:
    a) Scoop each Basic Beat in each measure.
    b) Write the Basic Beat below the Scoop.
    c) Write the Pulse below each Basic Beat.
    d) Write the Counts below each Pulse.

♪ **Ti-Do Time:** TAP the Basic Beat with your foot while you CLAP each rhythm.
COUNT out loud while you TAP and CLAP.

TAP with TI-DO in 4/4 TIME

In $\frac{4}{4}$ Time, there are 4 quarter note Basic Beats (4 counts) in each measure.

1. Add a rest below each bracket to complete each measure in $\frac{4}{4}$.

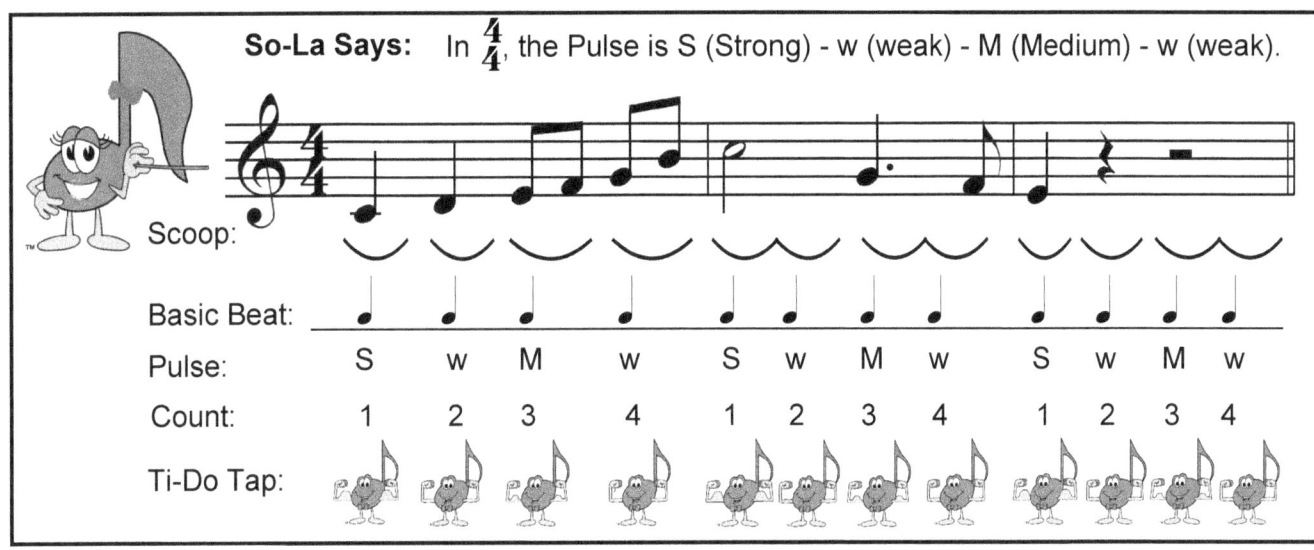

♫ **Ti-Do Tip:** UPPER case letter for **S** (Strong) and **M** (Medium); and lower case letter for **w** (weak).

2. Following the Example:
   a) Scoop each Basic Beat in each measure.
   b) Write the Basic Beat below the Scoop.
   c) Write the Pulse below each Basic Beat.
   d) Write the Counts below each Pulse.

> ♫ **Ti-Do Time:** TAP the Basic Beat with your foot while you CLAP each rhythm.
> COUNT out loud while you TAP and CLAP.

Ultimate Music Theory
Level 2 Theory Exam

Total Score: ____
             100

The Ultimate Music Theory™ Rudiments Workbooks, Supplemental Workbooks and Exams prepare students for successful completion of the Royal Conservatory of Music Theory Levels.

1. a) Write the notes on the Bass Staff for the keys labeled with a ☺ on the keyboard. Use whole notes.
   b) Name the notes.
   c) Draw a line from each note to the corresponding key on the keyboard (at the correct pitch).

___
10

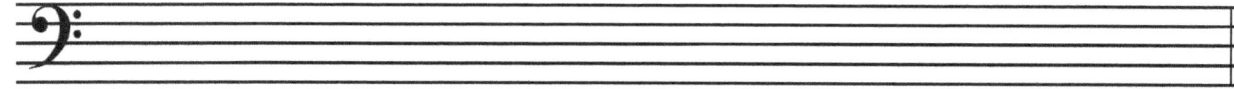

2. a) Write the note that is a whole step (whole tone) above each given note. Use a whole note.

___
10

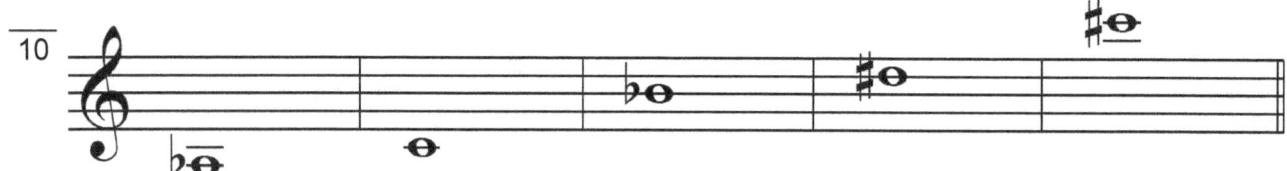

b) Write **W** below the whole steps (whole tones) and **H** below the half steps (semitones).

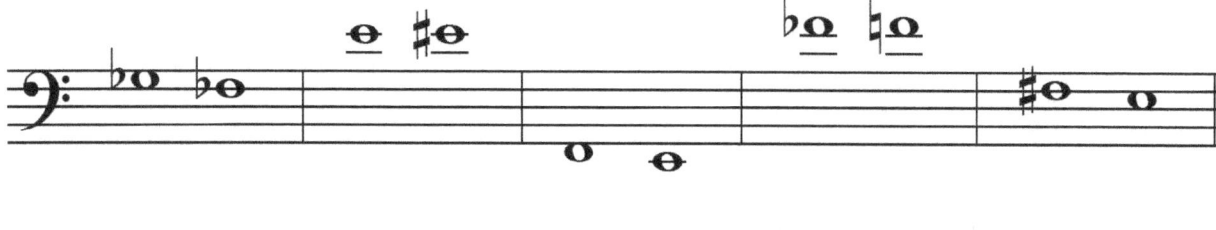

Ultimate Music Theory
Level 2 Theory Exam

3. a) Write the e minor harmonic scale, ascending and descending. Use a Key Signature and any necessary accidentals. Use whole notes.

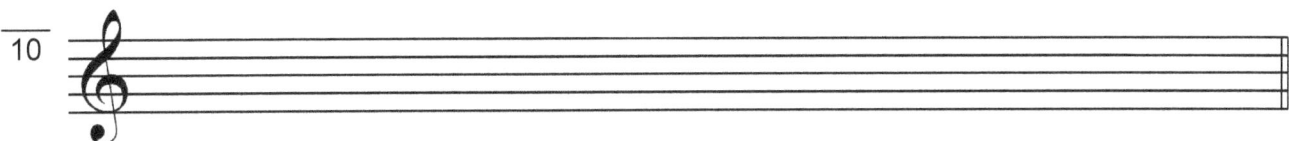

b) Write the G Major scale, ascending and descending. Use accidentals. Use whole notes.

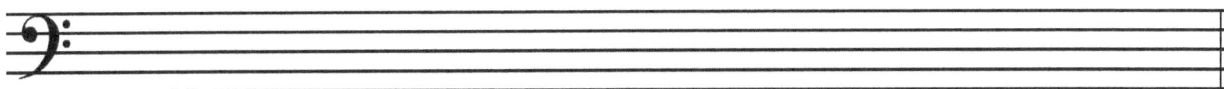

c) For the following d minor harmonic scale, label each Tonic (T), Subdominant (SD), Dominant (D) and Leading Tone (LT).

d) For the following d minor natural scale, label each Tonic (T), Subdominant (SD), Dominant (D) and Subtonic (SBT).

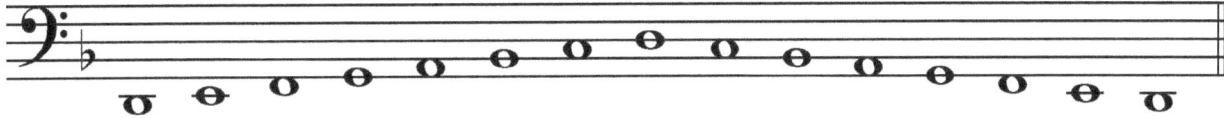

e) Name the following scale.

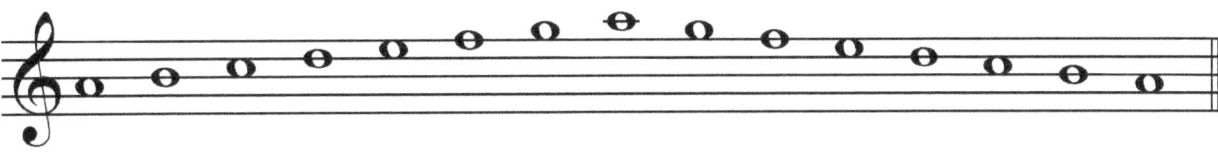

Scale: _____

Ultimate Music Theory
Level 2 Theory Exam

4. Write the following Tonic triads. Use a Key Signature. Use whole notes.

10   a) Tonic triad of e minor, solid   b) Tonic triad of G Major, broken descending

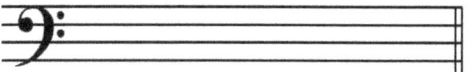 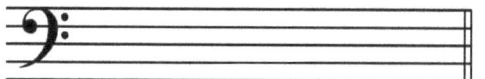

c) Tonic triad of C Major, solid   d) Tonic triad of d minor, broken ascending

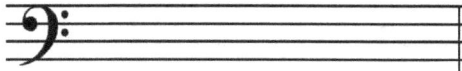 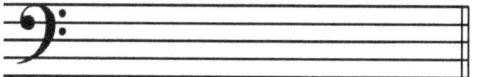

e) Tonic triad of F Major, broken, descending

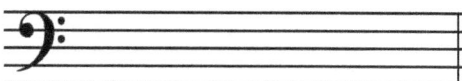

5. a) Add bar lines to complete the following rhythm.

b) Add a rest (or rests) below each bracket to complete each measure.

Ultimate Music Theory
Level 2 Theory Exam

6. For each Tonic triad:
    a) Name the Tonic Note and the Major or minor Key.
    b) Write the Functional Chord Symbol below the staff.
    c) Write the Root/Quality Chord Symbol above the staff.

10

Key: _____ ___   Key: _____ ___

Tonic: _____   Tonic: _____

Key: _____ ___   Key: _____ ___   Key: _____ ___

Tonic: _____   Tonic: _____   Tonic: _____

7. Name the size of the interval in each measure. Use interval numbers only.

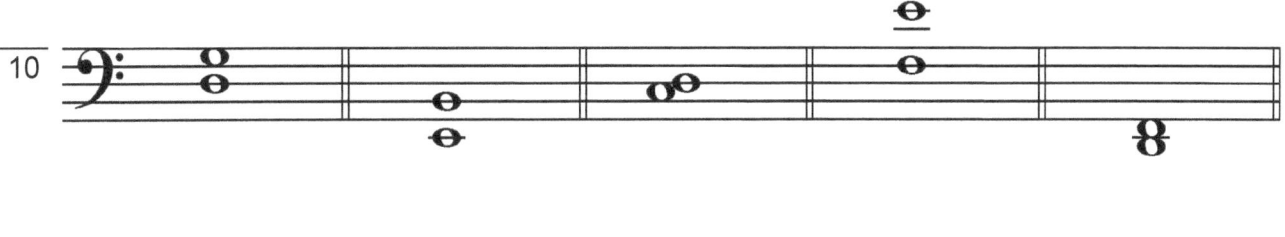

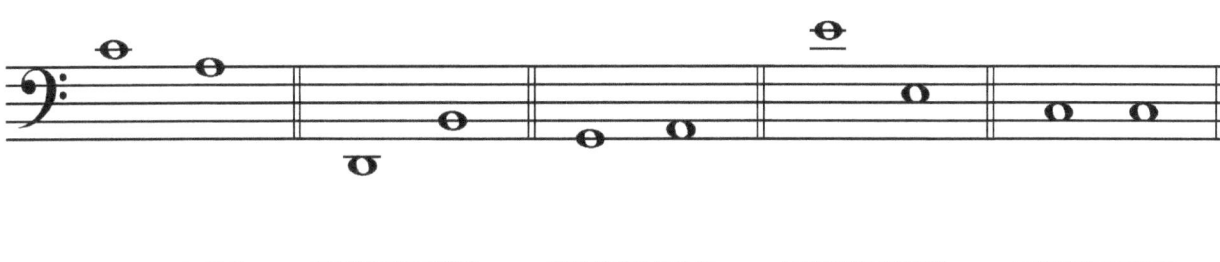

Ultimate Music Theory
Level 2 Theory Exam

8. The following questions are based on life and music of Wolfgang Amadeus Mozart. Check (✓) the correct answer (True or False) to each statement.

___
10

    a) Mozart was born in 1756 and composed his first piece at the age of 5.

        ☐ True   or   ☐ False

    b) Mozart composed 2 symphonies and 3 concertos.

        ☐ True   or   ☐ False

    c) The Third Movement of the Horn Concerto No. 4 in E flat Major, K 495 is in Rondo Form.

        ☐ True   or   ☐ False

    d) Mozart's Theme and Variations based on Twinkle, Twinkle, Little Star has 22 variations.

        ☐ True   or   ☐ False

    e) Mozart's favorite instrument was the French Horn.

        ☐ True   or   ☐ False

9. Write the Term for each of the following definitions. Do not use abbreviations or signs.

___
10   a) very soft   _____

       b) slowing down   _____

       c) very loud   _____

       d) very fast   _____

       e) much, very   _____

Ultimate Music Theory
Level 2 Theory Exam

10. Analyze the following piece of music by answering the questions below.

Twinkle Twinkle Little Star
Mozart

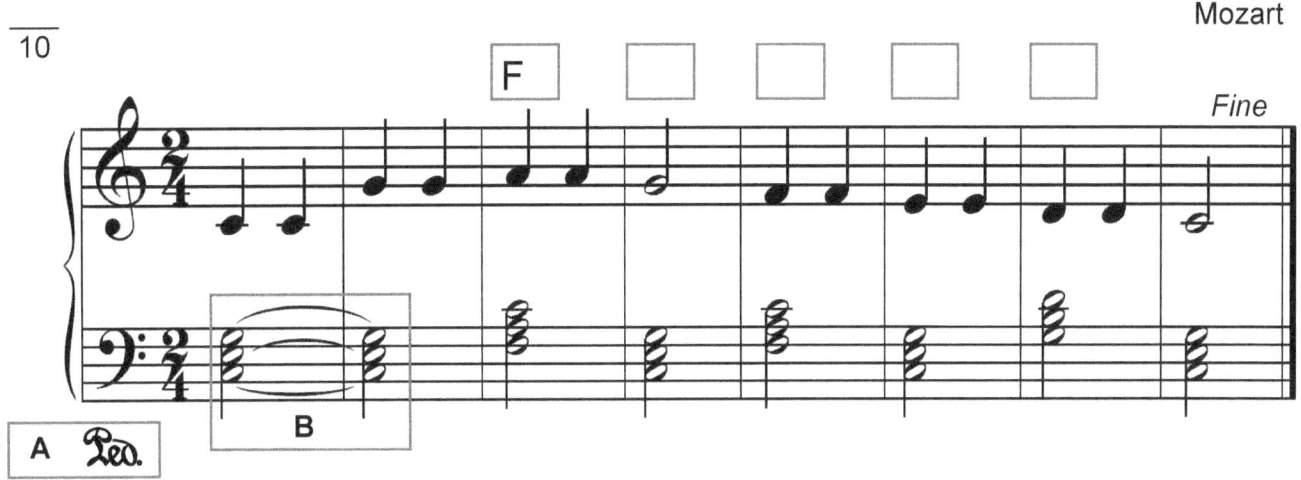

a) Explain the sign at the letter A. _____

b) Explain the sign at the letter B. _____

c) Write the Root/Quality Chord Symbol above the staff for measures 4 to 7.

d) Circle if the scale degree at the end of the phrase in measure 8 is: $\hat{1}$ OR $\hat{3}$

e) Circle if the repeated motive pattern at letter C and D is: repetition   OR   sequence

f) Explain the sign at the letter E. _____

g) Circle if the scale degree at the end of the phrase in measure 16 is: $\hat{2}$ OR $\hat{7}$

Bonus - Play "Twinkle Twinkle Little Star" on your instrument. Add So-La Sparkles to make it Twinkle!

Ultimate Music Theory Certificate

_____

has successfully completed all the requirements of the

Music Theory Level 2

_____ _____
Music Teacher *Date*

Enriching Lives Through Music Education

www.ingramcontent.com/pod-product-compliance
Lightning Source LLC
Chambersburg PA
CBHW081734100526
44591CB00016B/2613